The Change¹³

Insights into Self-Empowerment

Jim Britt ~ Jim Lutes

With

Co-authors from Around the World

The Change[13]

Jim Britt ~ Jim Lutes

All Rights Reserved
Copyright 2017

The Change
10556 Combie Road, Suite 6205
Auburn, CA 95602

The use of any part of this publication, whether reproduced, stored in any retrieval system, or transmitted in any forms or by any means, electronic or otherwise, without the prior written consent of the publisher, is an infringement of copyright law.

Jim Lutes ~ Jim Britt
The Change[13]

ISBN: 978-1-5323-3785-7

Co-authors

Jacqui Olliver

Dr. LeAnne Smith

Anthony G. Solimini Jr.

Rhoda Lipscomb

Casandra Carmine

Sharissa Sebastian

Scott Anthony Sadler

Margo Massard

Gina Grahame

Harry Nichols

Robin Rose

Chris Meyers Moore

Molly McGee Hewitt

Doug Herold

Christie Garcia

Evelyn Wang

Susan Sharp

Chad Steven

Angela Barrows

Bernie Garrett

The Change is proud to support Good Women International.

Every five minutes, one American child (many as young as ten years old) will be abducted and trafficked into the sex trade. 274 children a day, 100,000 each year and that estimate could be low. The total current number of human trafficking victims in the U.S. alone reaches into the hundreds of thousands and worldwide into the millions.

All profits from the sale of Amazon Kindle electronic books are being donated to Good Women International, whose focus is on the prevention of sexual exploitation of young women and children. They support self-empowerment and educational programs worldwide designed to educate our youth to avoid becoming a victim. A recent successful project was an anti-trafficking curricula for our high schools which is now complete and being utilized in many high schools around the world.

Enslavement is a reality. It is documented and it is real. The question is: What are we going to do about it?

To make a donation to Good Women International, a non-profit subsidiary of Village Care International, go to: www.SupportGoodWomen.com. All donations are tax deductible under Tax ID #: 88-0471768. We welcome and appreciate your donations, no matter how small.

http://GoodWomenInternational.org

Note: *Donations are never for salaries, as Good Women is a volunteer organization.*

DEDICATION

This book is dedicated to all those seeking change

Foreword

Berny Dohrmann, Chairman of CEO Space International

To The Readers of *The Change* Series:

Jim Britt has been a mentor to *Chicken Soup* authors, and to some of the foremost thought leaders on earth. Jim Britt's groundbreaking work in *Letting Go*, releasing past traumas and betrayals in life to return once again to forward-looking manifestation within your full powers, has been instructing at leading *Fortune* companies and to standing-room-only seminars all over the world. For three decades, Jim Britt has been the "trainer of the trainers," of which I am only one. Jim has been an instructor at CEO Space, the most prestigious, hard to get into faculty on the planet, where he developed millions of dollars of resources as he assisted others to develop tens of millions of dollars for their own dream making. Jim is the most "unchanged by success and wealth" man I have ever known. He is an unselfish archangel, like in his book *Rings of Truth*.

Today, Jim Britt and Jim Lutes, along with many inspiring co-authors from around the world, bring a pioneering work to the market to transform your own journey into master manifestation. Their principles are forged on coaching millions on every continent. As you read, you are exploring self-development as the world has yet to practice. In fact, Jim and Jim's publications lead to this one APEX MOMENT. Everything you have done to date in your own life, everyone you have met, every lesson you have learned, has led you to this one GREAT life opportunity… the moment of your own transformation into ever-rising full potentials.

As a five-time best-selling author myself, as a filmmaker, and with CEO Space, you can imagine how fussy I am to write a foreword to publications in the self-development space. CEO Space was just ranked by *Forbes Magazine* as the leading entrepreneur firm, which hosts five annual business growth conferences serving over 140 countries. It was also named by *Forbes* as THE MEETING in the world that YOU CANNOT AFFORD TO MISS. The world today demands more than a reputation defender to secure your forward brand; it requires that you take responsibility for your own brand and reputation in life. This book will inspire you to do just that.

CEO Space International has supported launches for many amazing works, including *Chicken Soup for the Soul; Men Are From Mars, Women Are From Venus; Rich Dad, Poor Dad; The Secret; No Matter What; Three Feet From Gold; Conversations With The King*; and now the movies *Growing Up Graceland* and *Wish Man* (for Make a Wish Foundation); *Outwitting the Devil* by Napoleon Hill and Sharon Lechter; Tony Robbins' great publications; of course Jim Britt's best-selling book *Rings of Truth;* and so many more. The totals have reached more than 2 billion eyeballs! You can't play around with that Mount Everest of credibility that I guard like a bank vault!

You can therefore appreciate why I encourage 100% of our followers of all the publications named to BUY JIM BRITT and JIM LUTES' book series *The Change* as a customer recognition for your own ten-best close relationships or clients. But don't just buy this book; rather, I endorse that you buy 10, and you giftwrap them to acknowledge your most important top ten relationships in life or clients in business. By doing so, you will retain more clients and encourage repeat buying. You may also receive more referrals and strengthen each relationship. The laws of giving will come back to you 10 to 1. When you give freely, you will always receive a rain into your life just as you rain into the lives of those you treasure. Jim Britt, Jim Lutes, and the insightful and inspiring co-authors have given you in *The Change* series a great opportunity... more important than pouring ice water over someone's head on YouTube as a challenge for charity! The gift that keeps on giving begins when you step up and BUY 10, knowing you have been instrumental in inspiring 10 friends to live a better life. Together, we are going to reach 1 BILLION SOULS as we help Jim Britt, Jim Lutes, and their co-authors to achieve their goal to transform human consciousness in our lifetime. Like Zig Ziglar, Jim Rohn, the great Roger Anthony, and so many friends who have passed, my friend Jim Britt is now a historical event in every training, every publication, and every online work at CEO Space. If you ever have the opportunity, STOP YOUR LIFE and see JIM BRITT & JIM LUTES LIVE and you will thank me personally, I know.

Their work is powerful. You'll let go of the baggage you've been carrying around for years and learn to embrace everything that creates the future you want and deserve. As you close the pages of any of *The Change* books, you will say over and over again "THANK YOU Jim Britt and Jim Lutes for creating this work." You will gain a new life of super focus as never before and you will commence to master manifest in your own individual life as never before. *The Change* books provide tools to transform results for corporations, institutions, and individuals, and once applied it will be impossible to miss your future success in life.

In my opinion, there are only the following areas to embrace for each of us:

Spiritual oneness and balance

Recreational balance and nature

Relationship where *Perfection Can Be Had!* (my book)

Career attainment of goals that you, yourself, reset along the way

Parenting either directly or by embracing a child you adopt to mentor at any and every age in life

These perspectives come into alignment within the framework of Jim Britt and Jim Lutes' imagination, along with decades of human-potential work. My advice is this work is a "BUY 10 TO SHARE WITH FRIENDS" pledge. In fact, a billion readers is a global path that Jim Britt and Jim Lutes are going to achieve NEXT for the world common good.

Let's help in this quest, as both men unselfishly donate their only asset, their precious LIFE TIME, to elevate one life at a time to their full potential and greatness.

My final request to all those who are reading my foreword is that you DO IT NOW. When you think of the good you will be doing, just ask yourself, "How long will I make them WAIT?"

I'm buying my 10 today!

Berny Dohrmann

Chairman, CEO Space International

P.S. I so approve this message for all my readers and followers worldwide. CEO Space has helped authors break the book of all records a half a dozen times, which means the only record to beat can be done with the publication you are buying 10 of now. Together, we are going to set a global record with one publication. Make the PLEDGE and give the gift of personal development. DO IT TODAY!

Table of Contents

Foreword ix

Jim Britt 1
   Overcoming Self-Imposed Money Limitations

Jim Lutes 9
   Internal Influence

Chris Meyers Moore 23
   The Only Lasting Truth Is Change

Christie Garcia 37
   Create Your Impact

Anthony G. Solimini Jr. 49
   How M&M's Changed My Life

Bernie Garrett 59
   Armed for Success

Jacqui Olliver 71
   Vital, Problem Free Sex Education

Evelyn Wang 83
   Bridging The Divide Within

Scott Sadler 97
   5 Mindful Questions That Lead to Success

Chad Steven 109
   Accomplishment Through Action

Dr. Rhoda Lipscomb 119
   The Winds of Change Regarding Sexuality

Dr. LeAnne N. Smith 129
   The Art of Being F.A.K.E. The Secrets to the Mastery of Self-Actualization

Angela Barrows 143
   You Have a Choice. So Choose to Stop Struggling

Casandra Carmine 155
   Take a Step Left, Victim to Victor

Doug Herold 167
   Personal Development

Gina Grahame 177
   Be the Hero of Your Own Life! Change Your Narrative and You'll Change Your Life

Margo Massard 189
   Being Me

Robin Rose 199
   A Scientific Approach to Healthy Self-Talk

Molly McGee Hewitt 211
   "The E Factor:" The Power of Encouragement

Sharissa Sebastian 221
   Mindset Makeover

Susan Sharp 233
   You're Already a Masterpiece

Harry Nichols 243
   Thought Modeling - The Heart Gateway Approach

Afterword 255

Jim Britt

Jim Britt is an internationally recognized leader in the field of peak performance and personal empowerment training. He is author of 13 best-selling books, including *Cracking the Rich Code; Cracking the Life Code; Rings of Truth; The Power of Letting Go; Freedom; Unleashing Your Authentic Power; Do This. Get Rich-For Entrepreneurs; The Flaw in The Law of Attraction;* and *The Law of Realization*, to name a few.

Jim has presented seminars throughout the world sharing his success principles and life-enhancing realizations with thousands of audiences, totaling over 1,000,000 people from all walks of life.

Jim has served as a success counselor to over 300 corporations worldwide. He was recently named as one of the world's top 20 success coaches and presented with the best of the best award out of the top 100 contributors of all time to the direct selling industry.

Jim is more than aware of the challenges we all face in making adaptive changes for a sustainable future.

Overcoming Self-Imposed Money Limitations
By Jim Britt

One of my favorite analogies that most of us at one time or another can identify with making money…or the lack of, is about the determined fly.

You've no doubt witnessed a fly beating its head against a window trying desperately to get to freedom. It's a life-or-death futile attempt to fly through the glass. You can tell by the sound that in his mind he's thinking "I must try harder." But it's just not working! Or maybe a fly can't think…but you get the picture.

No matter how hard it tries, we both know that the fly will never break through the glass and is doomed to die. We also know with just a few seconds of flying in the right direction, it could be free from its self-imposed trap…and with only a fraction of the effort. Yet he continues to beat his head against the glass until he dies. Without a doubt this approach makes sense to the fly - otherwise he would stop!

This is how most people feel when it comes to making more money. No matter how hard they try, they end up year after year with a repeat performance of the last, and in the end with barely enough to survive.

While it does require some effort, the point is that trying harder is not always the solution to earning more. They say that "persistence and practice makes perfect" but that's not altogether true if you are trying harder persisting and practicing the wrong thing like the fly.

Let's face it. Most of us from time to time feel that life is just one big financial struggle with a series of never ending money problems. Yet the truth is that life does not have to be that way. In fact, it can be just the opposite.

Earning more should not be about struggle. Earning more is about pursuing and creating what we truly desire in an easy, stress-free manner. Think about it. Which is easier, struggle to earn more, or having all you want?

Let me ask you a serious question: Do you really want to earn more but it seems to elude you? And why is it that it seems like such a struggle to create the things we want anyway?

Here's the real answer: If you are not earning all the money you want it is because your subconscious holds some contradictory intentions. In other words, you want something and your subconscious tells you that you are not capable based on past experiences.

For example, you might say, "I want to earn more money," but your dominant subconscious belief may be, "Earning the amount of money I want seems impossible." Or "My past experience says I have tried many times and failed."

Notice anything different about these statements? Of course! One program wants more and the other says it's impossible. That's what creates the struggle.

You are going in different directions. It's like driving your car with one foot on the accelerator and the other on the break and wondering why you are not getting anywhere.

So, what is this "Subconscious mind" that seems so mysterious? The conscious mind is simply the one you are using to read this article, or to make decisions about your life affairs. The subconscious mind is your programming…the sum total of your experiences in life. It is designed to protect you from repeating past mistakes by offering you feedback on a decision you are ab out to make. You touch a flame as a child and you get burned. Now when you get near a flame, your subconscious brings up the past experience and you know not to touch the flame. This all happens as an automatic subconscious response that never even registered in your conscious mind.

The reality is, because of past programming, past experiences, your conscious and subconscious are almost always in conflict. You <u>consciously</u> say, "I want more money" and then after listening, your <u>subconscious</u> checks in and says, "Hold on a minute. Money was hard to get as a child, or you lost everything before so you don't need to try again," or whatever. So it concludes that "No matter what you do, it is too difficult to create that amount of money". As a result, there is no agreement to make a change and they cancel each other out and therefore you give up on creating more money.

What's important to understand is that the two different agendas are creating an emotion or feeling that actually attracts that which you do not desire instead of what you do desire.

Let me explain to you what is really happening.

Once a firm decision is made to have more money (doesn't matter how much) the message is sent to the subconscious and it is carried out with precision, unless an old program is brought forth offering conflicting information. This is where you have to become consciously aware of the input from your subconscious. You make a decision, and immediately you start having doubt, you have to stop, let go of the doubt, so that your subconscious continues to act upon the decision you made rather than the doubt.

Remember, the Law of Cause and Effect is always working, you just have to become aware that it is working to your advantage or not.

Once a decision is made, one that doesn't allow for anything less, what you have firmly decided begins its journey back to you. It is no longer susceptible to any argument whatsoever. The subconscious mind cannot argue. It only acts. It accepts the conclusions of the conscious mind as final. So the point is that you have to consciously override what the subconscious is telling you, just like pushing "Delete" on your computer.

To put it simply, every decision you make has its own energetic vibrational harmony. That decision is impressed onto your subconscious mind. Then, through the Law of Cause and Effect it will energetically bring into your view people, opportunities, situations, etc. that has a vibrational harmony that matches yours.

So when you receive what you don't want, it simply means that your conscious decision has been overridden by a conflicting belief. Why? Because the decision was not a firm one that sent a firm signal to the subconscious.

If you send a "Half Baked" decision, "I am going to give this business a try and see if it works" what decision are you sending your subconscious to create. What vibrational harmony are you creating? When you look at what you are receiving you know exactly what you are sending.

Your subconscious mind cooperates completely with your conscious decision when it *understands* and *agrees* with what you consciously want. In other words, when the decision is firm, your conscious and subconscious are not in conflict.

So what do you do to change? First, decide what it is you want…a decision that doesn't allow for anything less. Then begin to consciously observe when you are feeling any emotional conflict. That is your inner guidance telling you that you are not acting in harmony with your decision.

Once the decision is made, the next step to change is the act of self-observation. When you feel conflict, act as though you have come to an intersection with a red light flashing and a sign that reads "Right turn on red after stop." Then ask yourself before you proceed, "Is this action going to take me in the direction I want to go, or am I acting on old programming?"

If you do nothing else, remember that you MUST correct and STOP the negative influence IN THE MOMENT IT HAPPENS if you are serious about getting rid of the self-imposed limitation.

So, how would you rate your performance to date? Are you achieving the results you want with the effort you are expending? It's impossible to change if you don't do something in a different way.

The problem is that people most often go with the obvious. We rely on the same thinking, same habits and behaviors we've used in the past, productive or not, because it's what we know. In fact, most of us are like the fly on the window, trying harder and harder, doing more of the same and getting nowhere fast. We resist new approaches because they make us feel more at risk…more uncomfortable. Know this; Financial success is just outside your comfort zone. If you are not uncomfortable, you are most likely not making progress.

Make sure that you have a burning desire, backed by a firm decision, and an internal heat hot enough to move you past just wishful thinking. Let your vision and decision for a better future consume you and drive your actions. Only your vision, decision and your passion hold the power to allow you to go the distance. Let your (mind) decision and vision direct your actions and let your heart (passion) take charge of your move forward!

Decide what you are worth and then feed the feelings that fuel your passion, by letting go of what disempowers you. Then give yourself permission to go after what you want most. Give yourself permission to earn more. Let your deepest desires to be wealthy, direct you. Set your sites high enough so that you challenge yourself to live fully. Otherwise a part of you remains asleep, your talents remain hidden, your income remains the same and your performance becomes that of a constant state of struggle.

Let's make today just 1%, or more, better than yesterday. You in? Awesome!

***

To contact Jim:

www.JimBritt.com

www.PowerOfLettingGo.com

www.CrackingTheRichCode.com

www.FaceBook.com/JimBrittOnline

Jim Lutes

Having taught his branded form of human performance since the early 1990s, Mr. Lutes has accelerated top-level entrepreneurs throughout his career by conducting trainings on personal growth and subconscious programming into worldwide markets.

During this time, Jim took his skills regarding the human mind, and combining it with trainings on influence, persuasion, and communication strategies, he launched Lutes International in the early 1990s. Based in San Diego, California, Jim has taught seminars for corporations, sales forces, individuals, and athletes. Having appeared on television, radio, and worldwide stages, Jim's style, knowledge, and effectiveness provide profound results.

"Jim Lutes possesses a unique ability to create performance change in an individual in a fraction of the time it takes his competitors." The core of human decisions is based on the programs we acquire, reinforce, and grow. Combining Jim's various trainings, individuals can reach new levels of achievement and fulfillment in all areas of life. The results are at times nothing short of astonishing.

Internal Influence

By Jim Lutes

Your vault - that is, the subconscious mind - stores a wealth of information for you. All of your experiences, emotions, memories, things you have learned, things you have heard, things your parents told you, messages from the media, messages from society. It's like an endless movie reel of data and information. All of this is in your subconscious mind and is therefore capable of influencing you in subtle and large ways. What is influencing you internally, or what I call your "internal influence," is impacting you more profoundly than you realize. The internal affects the external, so you can directly see the impact of your internal influence through what is happening to you and around you. Your internal influence is something to learn to be aware of – changing this will surely change what comes to you in your external environment.

There is one person you are with your whole life and that is you. Wherever you go, there you are. You are always with yourself. Keeping this in mind, are you aware of how you think? Have you noticed how you talk to yourself? Have you noticed how you react when you make a mistake, or things don't go your way? The tendency is to blame ourselves, or get mad at ourselves when we make mistakes. Of course, some people project the blame onto others, but don't be fooled – they are still blaming themselves. Many of these tendencies and cues have been gathered throughout the course of your life via your subconscious mind. Your inner 'movie reel' collected all of your life experiences and all of those messages and then designed a script that runs in your head. This script is married to that sense of safety and predictability that we talked about earlier. It repeats information that it thinks will help you maintain a known identity, so that you do not have to experience stepping out into an unknown identity. Have you ever wanted to step outside of yourself completely? Have you accepted that this is not possible? Of course it's not possible to disengage from yourself completely. However, what *is* possible is that you can change this internal script! You can re-program the thoughts and ideas you loop internally to deeply affect life in every way imaginable! You, along with everyone else on the planet, have access to this magical portal. Yes, that's right, it's your subconscious.

This is neither about loving yourself, nor is it about ceasing to hate yourself. This is, however, about recognizing how you affect your behavior through your thoughts and beliefs and getting present to the fact that you do. The more you gain awareness of your conscious thoughts, the more you can rearrange those thoughts to be positive and affirming, signaling the same to your subconscious. This puts you on the path to becoming an ally to yourself instead of continuing to be your own adversary. If you are struggling and life is always miserable for you, take a look at your thoughts and you will find the root of your struggle. If you think you can't change your thoughts, think again. The choice between remaining a victim of limiting thoughts and beliefs or freeing yourself from these limiting thoughts and beliefs actually exists, and it's yours to be made. You are responsible for your internal environment, and therefore your external environment. Your internal environment greatly affects your life circumstances. In fact, your willingness and ability to relate, connect to and design your interior life, by getting to know your own mind, is critical to changing your life circumstances. The trick is to learn how to get your subconscious on board, how to build and maintain that sturdy bridge between your conscious and subconscious minds with you as the director shifting in the direction of your dream life.

Despite all of the Universal Power accessible to us through the subconscious mind, it remains that the subconscious mind still contributes to holding us back. For, in that storehouse of all our experiences are also found all the patterns and beliefs that were given to us without our choosing them. I'm talking about all of the experiences you've had over the course of your lifetime. The subconscious mind, just like a sponge, has absorbed all of them. Whether from traumatic experiences during childhood or the programming from authority figures in your life, the majority of beliefs and patterns running from your subconscious were most definitely not chosen by you. What you can choose, however, is what thoughts are entering your conscious mind. You can become the discerning bouncer of the nightclub of your mind. The subconscious mind wants to make manifest that which the conscious mind is thinking, so the faster you get this concept and start working hard to armor your conscious mind with positive thoughts, the more you will be able to attract and create that which you desire.

It is important to distinguish who you really are in all of this. Are you your subconscious mind? Are you your conscious mind? Are you your identity (which was created out of your past and survival programming)? Are you your ego?

The ego is created from the first memories and events of your conscious mind. It is thus created from the outset, and, also from the outset, the ego created a barrier between you and the innate wisdom stored within the subconscious mind. Your ego rooted and solidified as your life wore on, and your patterns manifested as expected. You developed a set of characteristics and qualities that corresponded with your ego. This is mostly because you probably knew nothing else as you grew up, other than to perpetuate the patterns absorbed by the subconscious mind throughout your childhood. These patterns and programs are filled with defense strategies that are generated automatically whenever there is a threat to our identity. The ego is attached to the identity, commonly known as ego-identity, which makes the ego also not the full picture of who you really are. This is because you are not your identity! And you are not your ego. And you are not your ego-identity.

Contrary to popular belief, the voice in your head is also not you. The voice in your head is only a part of you. All the voice in your head knows it sees through the filter of the programming in your subconscious mind. We tend to trust the voice in our heads immensely, but it is not the seat of true wisdom, for any of us. The voice in our head, what I will call ego, operates on the plane of logic and rational thinking, but is unable to access the more creative and wise aspects of the subconscious mind. The ego is a mechanism devised to help you survive through life on the physical plane. Much of our ego is constructed around a set of beliefs and ideas that are a direct result of our conditioning and our experiences. These, as we know, are formed largely as a result of external information and cues from those around us. The ego helps you interact with people and your experiences, like a mental point of reference or template. The ego also keeps the myth of separation alive for all of us. It tries to convince us that we are not all part of the universal ocean of oneness. The ego likes words like 'me' and 'mine' and it filters your experience through the smallest universe possible, the universe of 'me'.

Without being able to separate ourselves from our egos, we will never truly be able to see that we are entirely one with the universe. The ego is tenacious! It is as though it has vested interest in convincing us that we do not have access to that infinite Universal Power that each of us does. How do we separate our sense of selves from our ego? Yes, you guessed it – by cultivating self-awareness. As we identify and recognize those underlying messages that come from our conditioning, we can begin to see that they are not actually who we are. You can relate to the ego as a necessary "cloak" of identity that enables you to be in relationship with yourself and with others, but never mistake it for your true *essence*. Through developing self-awareness, becoming aware of your own thoughts, patterns and habits, and then actively choosing to replace the old programming with newer supportive information, you can shift your relationship to your own ego. You remove the ego from the driver's seat! By doing this, we put our connection to Universal Power, our sense of ourselves as omnipotent in front of the wheel. When we take the ego out of the driver's seat, we give ourselves the opportunity to build a stronger connection to our subconscious mind, that limitless vault of Universal Power.

Tangled up in our manufactured identities and the surviving ego is our self-esteem. We often seek help improving our self-esteem and self-image by reading books, or turning to programs developed and run by experts in personal development. What I have learned in my years of personal development work is that the only way to improve self-esteem and self-image in a deeper, more integrated way is by turning to world-class subconscious reprogramming techniques. We must connect to and re-wire our subconscious mind in order to create a new foundation for our lives. This is the seat of our access to change and our ability to shift the course of our lives. There is no self-help book in the world that you can just read that will suddenly give you high self-esteem. You have to practice and implement the techniques daily, regardless of the book, program or teacher, in order to affect change. When you choose to work with your subconscious mind, however, you will get more effective results much faster. It's like choosing to fuel your car with the highest octane, purest source of gas versus going for the usual, run-of-the-mill unleaded variety. Sustainable, potent and rapid change comes from choosing and committing to work directly with your subconscious. When you do this, your life course changes rapidly and with more ease. Simple, effective, world-class tools and techniques will be revealed to you so that you can begin to chart the course of your life according to your wishes and dreams!

Having a healthy self-esteem begins in your childhood. Self-esteem is about how we value ourselves. It determines how we perceive our value to the world and how valuable we think we are to others. Self-esteem affects so many parts of our lives including our trust in others, our relationships, our work – virtually every part of our lives is impacted by how we bring ourselves to each interaction. Self-esteem is a core part of the mechanism that directly influences our sense of belonging, and how we relate to others. Self-esteem is directly connected to our sense of self-respect, and self-satisfaction and is expressed as having a sense of confidence. There is a spectrum of self-esteem states, and we can shift between them, from one to another. Positive self-esteem gives us the strength and flexibility to be the ones in charge of our lives. Positive self-esteem supports our ability to grow, our capacity for resilience and enables us to move beyond fear of rejection, and view mistakes as opportunities for growth.

On the other side of the spectrum is poor or low self-esteem. Authority figures in our lives, parents, teachers and bosses had a huge impact on how our self-esteem developed. If you were raised with parents who neglected you, boom! There goes your self-esteem. If you were raised with parents who doted on you, boom! There goes your self-esteem in the opposite direction. If you had the parent of the opposite sex treat you differently in any way, this can affect your self-esteem. Particularly if you are a woman and your father did not help you cultivate your self-image, your self-esteem may not have risen to the level it should be. If you went to school and your teachers made a comment that you were not smart, boom! There goes your self-esteem.

Sometimes the example of a balloon is used to illustrate our self-esteem. When we receive excessive praise or admiration for work that we have done, our self-esteem can over-inflate, like a balloon with too much air or helium inside. People with excessive self-esteem can become boastful or smug, sometimes trying to convince others of their own superiority. When we take in excessive criticism or hurtful comments about our work, or behavior, we can develop poor self-esteem, like a deflated balloon. Having poor self-esteem can make us feel as though we don't have value in the world and that the work we do doesn't matter. Sometimes this can lead to self-destructive or self-defeating behaviors. No matter what the interaction, how big or small, your emotional reaction at the time of the experience would have been felt by the subconscious mind and the memory of this is still held in your vault. These memories contributed to you having a healthy balanced self-esteem, an excessively high self-esteem or a poor or low self-esteem. Each of these conditions has an immense impact on how we perceive ourselves in the world, influencing our sense of value or sense of worthlessness. What can you do about this? First, as I've mentioned previously, you must determine where your self-esteem is on the self-esteem spectrum. Then, decide to change your self-esteem back to a higher, but balanced place. How? You reprogram your subconscious mind, giving you access to the memory that initially helped to create your self-esteem, and then, by separating out the emotion that was initially attached to the experience. You want to be able to have the memory, but to have it in a more neutral way, without so much emotion 'clouding' your memory of the experience. When you remove the emotion from the experience, you give yourself the opportunity for a new perspective of who you are, and thus enabling you to directly increase your self-esteem.

Why is good self-esteem important, anyway? I know, it's a rhetorical question. Self-esteem is directly related to our internal set of expectations about ourselves. Good self-esteem is what will get you to take action in your life – and you only get results by taking action. I mean it when I say that there is absolutely no use for low self-esteem. Low self-esteem serves to keep you stuck in limiting patterns and perpetuates the victim mentality. Low self-esteem keeps you stuck in the mailroom when you belong in the corner office with big windows. Low self-esteem keeps you single when you know you have a lot of love to give and deserve a healthy relationship. It serves no one – and you serve no one when you are indulging in it. And yes, it is actually indulgent to wallow in a perpetual sense of self-esteem!

That's right – I said it is indulgent to be stuck in low self-esteem. This is because ultimately, like anything, low self-esteem is a choice. If you suffer from low self-esteem, although you certainly did not choose to be imprinted with it or grow up with the experiences you had that created it, you are in your present life also not choosing to overcome it. This is how it limits you. If you really understand that you can choose to have high self-esteem, that having low self-esteem is not a curse or something you cannot erase and undo, then you can do the work you need to do to raise your self-esteem. Low self-esteem is not part of your DNA! When you consider the true nature of who you are, as something that emerged from Universal Power and is connected to Universal Power, the very notion of self-esteem at all is entirely ridiculous! I'm offering but one channel for you to explore when seeking to raise your self-esteem, there are many. I know that subconscious mind reprogramming is the most effective because it cuts right to the core of the emotion behind the cause. You can set yourself free and be your own best friend just by raising your self-esteem. It is that simple. The techniques and methods in this book will show you how to do this.

Let's illustrate the two main expressions of self-esteem using an example. Let's say there is a set of twins, Sam and Shelley. When the twins were nine, their parents divorced and Sam went to live with his mother, Karen, and Shelley went to live with her father, Hank. Karen was a successful life insurance sales broker, breaking sales records many years in a row. She was raised in a loving family and had great relationships with her family and friends. Karen remained single for a couple of years following her divorce from Sam and Shelley's dad. Everyone who ran into her remarked on her poise, grace, friendliness and sense of confidence. Shelley loved being a parent and she and Sam had great relationship, even into

Sam's early teenage years. Sam was successful at school, held a part-time job and even ran for school president.

Hank married his mistress as soon as his divorce with Sam and Shelley's mom went through. Hank's new wife, Roberta was much younger than Karen. At first, Shelley really liked living with her dad. He paid a lot of attention to her, praised her academic achievements and her success on sports teams, and devoted time to parenting her to the best of his ability. As Shelley moved into her teenage years, Hank began to spend all of his time with Roberta and his job and completely neglected his role as a doting father. At the same time, her grades began to slip, she quit her sports teams and she began having one boyfriend after another, not spending much time with her girlfriends. When Shelley began to fail a couple of her classes, her guidance counselor called her in to talk to her about her grades, her truancy and eventually they got to the topic of her self-esteem. In talking with the school counselor, Shelley discovered that she had very low self-esteem and that this was contributing to her difficulty in school, her difficulty in her social circles and her lack of enthusiasm for the sports teams she used to love. When her father turned his full attention onto his new wife, Shelley's self-esteem plummeted. She tried to counter this loss of investment by her father through having relationships with boyfriends. Once Shelley and her counselor became aware of the origin of some of her poor self-esteem, she was sent back to the guidance counselor to address it. Shelley worked with the guidance counselor to understand how her mind had developed feelings of inadequacy, through experiencing her father's neglect. Shelley's counselor helped Shelley to understand that she had allowed her own mind to turn against herself, thus eroding her capacity for success at school, in her social circles and, most importantly, her sense of place and value in the world. Shelley's counselor explained to her that she could actually reprogram her mind with more supportive and empowering thoughts, feelings and ideas, so that she could replace the limiting beliefs with ones that nourished her success. She explained to Shelley that she could in fact, become her own best friend.

Why wouldn't you want to be your own best friend? You are with yourself 24/7, 365! Imagine if, instead of being angry with yourself for running late all the time, you had nothing but acceptance and compassion for yourself? Chances are, with acceptance and compassion for yourself you would eventually turn your late behavior into punctuality. What if, instead of being hard on yourself for eating that donut, you just ate the donut and were happy about it? Chances are the donut will process much more easily through your digestive system – and you will be less likely to reach for a second one. I'm not even asking you to love yourself – although it's pretty close! You can fake it until you make it, as they say, when it comes to growing your self-esteem. If you have to look in the mirror daily and tell yourself how awesome you are, then so be it. You could also reprogram your subconscious mind and replace days and months and years of repeating positive affirmations with one session using the right tools and techniques – like the ones we'll discuss in chapter eleven.

When you switch your internal influence paradigm from being one where you constantly belittle yourself to one where you are your own cheerleader, you will see the benefits immediately. It is a total waste of time to remain in low self-esteem, especially because there are effective methods for raising it. Low self-esteem may serve you because chances are it keeps you out of trouble, keeps you comfortable and perhaps even keeps you feeling safe. It may feel comfortable to remain in a place of low self-esteem because the thought of change creates a strong sense of fear for you. If you have low self-esteem and let it keep you from taking action, then guess what? You are avoiding your life! Staying in low self-esteem lets you be complacent, it absolves you of responsibility and it helps you avoid fear. You take no risks when you take no action. You don't grow, you don't move yourself forward and you don't challenge yourself to keep improving. You become like water that has become stagnant, and we all know what stagnant water smells like!

Low self-esteem is a self-perpetuating state of being, and until you actively seek to overcome it, you will be living a life that is completely cut off from achieving what you want, paralyzed by low self-esteem. Further, you will constantly be wallowing in a state of self-hate, and then you will find that you are no fun to be with – and here you are, stuck with yourself all the time. Think about what keeps you in low self-esteem. Take a good look around you at everyone else and see who is taking action and who isn't. Some of those do-ers don't even have high self-esteem –yet. But the very fact of their willingness to take action is leading them in the right direction. Take a step in the direction of raising your self-esteem and you will see how the universe will rise up to show you how big you can really go. Everything you want in the world – including a new and improved you – is waiting for you to activate it by clearing your subconscious mind and establishing positive thoughts in your conscious mind. This influences your self- esteem directly, and your expectations, and subsequently the actions you take in the world.

If low self-esteem is an unhelpful way to be, what is high self-esteem then? When you become your own best friend you pave the way for other people to love and accept themselves. You act from an empowered place, in alignment with your internal values. You are also more willing to take action to make things happen in your life. You are much less narcissistic than when you have low self-esteem. Believe it! All that time caught up in thinking you're worthless is really vain! People with high self-esteem want to serve others. They know that giving makes them feel good. They are going for their goals with love. They have a zest for life that is palpable. It's up to you which side you want to be on, but it is the people with high self-esteem that make things happen in the world. High self-esteem is such an important part of the process of developing your potential, of becoming the fullest expression of yourself!

It is not worth blaming your past, your parents, or whomever it might be that you hold responsible for having low self-esteem. It is, however, worth doing some personal work to increase your self-esteem so you can transcend all the negative and limiting stories you have been hanging onto and step into what you are really capable of in the world. Reprogramming your subconscious mind is a fast and effective way to get there, let me assure you. Your ability to influence yourself internally is huge, in fact, it's all there is. So it is vital that you get your internal influence aligned in a way that will serve you and your highest self and vision for your life. Your internal dialogue becomes the story you tell yourself every day, this is the voice that witnesses and reflects to you your perceptions of everything that happens to you in a day. This is your inner world, which translates directly into your outer world. This is where your power emanates from, and so many people nowadays don't grasp this concept. In the West, we live in a world that is constantly bombarding us with media, sounds, images, along with a whole multitude of external distractions. To take the time to become aware, to tune into and work with your subconscious mind effectively is the most powerful tool available to you. This is the only way you can change the course of your life and bring your goals into your reality.

So many people don't know this or don't see this and give away their power to others constantly. But your internal influence is your power, and you must learn to recognize and utilize your power to bring you all the good in the world that you desire. Begin to believe that you do hold that power within yourself! Stop playing small and keeping yourself out of the game! Grow your self-esteem, take risks and step into living large! Let me show you the steps and methods that will move you into this direction.

The only thing holding you back in this life is you. There is no better time than right now to choose to become your own best friend and cheerleader and influence yourself from the inside out in the most positive way possible.

***

To contact Jim:

Email: info@lutesinternational.com

Websites: www.lutesinternational.com

www.jimluteslive.com

Chris Meyers Moore

Chris Meyers Moore has had a distinguished career in media and marketing. Her focus now is sharing her blueprint for success as a motivational speaker. Audiences report, "She has changed my life".

She left the security of auto giant General Motors to start her media marketing company with offices in Detroit, Chicago and Los Angeles. Prestigious clients included: *The New York Times, CBS, Hearst Magazines, Conde Nast, Readers Digest and Forbes.*

Her accomplishments have been widely recognized. Advertising Age Magazine named her one of the "100 Top US Sales People." *Glamour* Magazine called her one of the Top Ten Working Women in America. *Media Decisions* Magazine put her on the cover. Her company was recognized by the National Association of Women Business Owners as one of the Top 10 Women Owned Businesses in Michigan. She is listed in Marquis Who's Who and Who's Who in American Business. Moore was named Michigan's Advertising Woman of the Year.

Chris is particularly proud of her work on behalf of women. She was asked to launch the Michigan chapter of the prestigious **International Women's Forum**, www.iwforum.org, a global foundation started to give prominent women a platform for networking. She was the recipient of the **Vanguard Award for Leadership** from **Women in Communications.**

The Only Lasting Truth Is Change

By Chris Meyers Moore

"If my critics saw me walking over the Thames they would say it was because I couldn't swim."

Margaret Thatcher, Former Prime Minister of Great Britain

Change. We don't need to define or prove it. It is a fact of life that everything in the infinite universe undergoes change. Constantly. There is no escaping it. So your goal is learning to cope with it and emerge stronger and better with a minimum of pain. Embracing change is what this book is all about. While change is universal and inevitable, it is also very personal as the vast spectrum of stories in this book will teach you. Here is mine.

I am a veteran of change—in my career as well as my personal life. I have a full range of battle scars from trying to be Superwoman, a woman for all seasons which means that much of my life has been about change.

　　* Balancing a high level corporate career at General Motors (which was the #1 car company in the world).

　　* Starting two companies—one a failure and the other a success so great that I never could have imagined I would be making personally a great deal of money year after year.

　　*Being served for divorce by my husband and falling in love with a New Yorker…that change resulted in a 12-year commuter marriage and 1.2 million frequent flier miles.

　　*Raising a highly-spirited daughter as a single Mother.

*Thriving as a senior citizen and a Yankee in the Old South with a new business venture and the same old New York husband 27 years later.

> *"When I let go of what I am, I become what I might be."*
>
> *-Lao Tzu, Chinese Philosopher 604 BC*

The philosophers tell us that we must embrace change. They are right, of course. Not just because it is inevitable but because it is far better to be the master of your destiny than the passive victim of someone else's desire for change. As Spencer Johnson put it succinctly in his book, *Who Moved my Cheese*, "A change imposed is a change opposed."

But just because change is the nature of things, it doesn't mean that we have to like it. In fact, most of us don't. I am a living breathing example.

I grew up in a loving stable family in a modest house in a close-knit neighborhood and walked to school holding my little sister's hand. I went to the University of Michigan just 40 miles from home then returned to begin my career. I married a local man and lived within a few miles of where I grew up. Looking back, I understand why New York husband jokingly nicknamed me the "Michigan Barnacle."

But it is also important to know that not all change is unpleasant, undesired, or unwelcome.

As women, it is fair to say that every one of us has promised to change--to lose weight, to stop smoking or to use sun screen when we go outdoors. We regularly make these New Year's resolutions, and with equal regularity we break them.

The reason is that recognizing the need for change is just the easy first step. The daunting difficulty is implementing change, which is why those New Year's resolutions fall in the waste basket of good intentions.

Why is implementation so difficult? Because we know that change is not without cost. We understand, either honestly and openly, or intuitively and subjectively, that change will hurt. Hurt yourself, your family, your children, and your business…all or some of the above.

Uncertainty and discomfort underlie change. We are always more comfortable with the known, which is the present, than the unknown—what if it turns out that I hate the new job, the new city, the new man? It makes sense that the greater the quantity and velocity of the changes, the greater the quantity and complexity of the problems associated with the change.

Or the bigger your life, the bigger your problems. I decided that I might as well accept that. That acceptance assuaged much of the pain.

The change I confronted was a nasty divorce and the upheaval that comes with it. This was a decision I knew I had to make. But my implementation was flawed. Actually, it was non-existent. We were the Barbie and Ken of the community with the perfect marriage. In my quintessential middle class Michigan suburb of America, after all, women do not leave their husbands. Much later I felt better to discover that wives initiate over 52% of divorces.

One of my worst fears was that my father would condemn me. But he surprised me when I told him I was getting divorced by saying, "What took you so long?" As for friends, I quickly learned who my true friends were.

A lesson learned is that you can't anticipate every result of change. Don't drive yourself crazy trying to predict every potential consequence. Instead, strive to remain resilient and ready to cope. I put that into practice and it worked for me.

My inability to quickly implement my decision had real unintended consequences. My husband finally realized, among our bickering, that our marriage had been over for some time and he exploded with rage.

The divorce was ugly (my husband wanted full custody of our daughter without visitation, alimony, child support and half of my company). It went on for too long (over 4 years), cost too much and almost lost me the love of my life who had about given up on me.

I would have been much better off to do what I had done so often in business, "Take the bull by the horns…" Get it over with and move on.

> *"Some changes look negative on the surface but you will soon realize that space is being created in your life for something new to emerge."*
>
> *---Eckhart Tolle, Canadian Author,*
> *The Power of Now*

It sounds Pollyannaish but Tolle is correct, and his advice is worth remembering.

Based on my personal experiences at home and in the office, I formulated four maxims that have helped me along the way. Now I would like to share them. Put into practice, they will help you broaden your horizons and fortify you against the inevitable "slings and arrows of outrageous fortune" that Shakespeare wrote about so eloquently.

Change #1 Stop apologizing.

Apologizing doesn't mean that you stop saying the words "I'm sorry" or "excuse me" or "oops, I made a mistake." That's just good manners. But apologizing for being smart; for being successful; for being powerful is insidiously destructive because it goes to the core of our being…of what we think about ourselves.

What underlies most women's apologies and what I have heard too often coming from women's lips, including my own, is some version of "please forgive me for sounding so intelligent, or smart or for getting that job."

For instance, when I was being recruited for the executive position of Advertising Manager of Pontiac division of General Motors, by Jim Graham, Marketing Director of Pontiac, the man who became my boss, I said: "Do you think I can handle this job? I mean there has never been a woman in that position before. I have never overseen a $300 million-dollar budget."

In effect, I was apologizing for not being qualified. Thank goodness Jim Graham did not agree. And he hired me. That job changed my life and ultimately my career path forever.

Later after the newspaper stories and magazine articles, people would congratulate me then ask, "How in the world did you get that job?" The unspoken inference was intelligence wasn't the skill that got me hired. The fact was that I had been a Super Star as the promotion director of Hudson's Department Stores, then a Midwest giant. One of my promotions even made the Guinness Book of Records.

At that time, conventional wisdom said that car people were car people and clothes people certainty could not be car people. Fortunately for me, Graham was a visionary who believed in transferable skills.

So, as a well-schooled second class citizen, aka woman, I would mumble something about being so thankful my husband was very supportive and made it all possible. I was such a skilled actress that my family and our friends believed that he was the bread winner when, in fact, his company was not successful.

This attitude of "I am not good enough" affects many women from the top of the ladder on down. A study published in 2017 in the journal *Science* found that girls as young as 6 years old already believed that boys are more "brilliant." The gender stereotype is still pervasive.

Even Virginia Rometty, IBM's first female CEO speaks of being offered a "big job" early on in her career and worrying, like I did, that she did not have the requisite skills. Later, when discussing the offer with her husband, he pointed out, "Do you think a man would have ever answered that question that way?" The answer was—and is— a resounding "No!"

> *"Believe in yourself! Have faith in your abilities! Without a humble, but reasonable confidence in your own power, you cannot be successful or happy."*
>
> *-Norman Vincent Peale, Minister, Author: The Power of Positive thinking*

I know from painful personal experiences that changing your perception of yourself does not come easily—or early on. Self-doubt lurks deep in our sub-consciousness as I discovered when I embarked on my "encore career" as a motivational speaker.

I could not come up with a topic. All I needed to do was to tell my story: that I was the only person in my family to graduate from college, that I became the highest-ranking woman in the global auto industry, that I left to start my media marketing company in the basement of my home, made lots of money, appeared on the cover of national magazines and was voted one of the Top 100 Sellers in the U.S. by Advertising Age Magazine. In short, I embraced change and completely re-made my personal and business life. I was a certified success and should be an inspiration for many women.

But when I tried to craft it into a speech I froze. In frustration, I joined the prestigious National Speakers Association and attended brainstorming sessions in the hopes of re-kindling my self-confidence. I realized I was uncomfortable with this "accomplishment generation" process.

Now I'm a seller and enthusiast at heart. I can pitch anything—from the attributes and benefits of selling sand to Saudis; ice to Eskimos, cosmetics to Mary Kay.

But I couldn't figure out how to sell myself.

I talked to a business coach friend of mine in New York who told me she had several female executive clients with this difficulty…but never one of her male clients. That's because women do not believe that success and likeability go hand in hand. We are taught to be likable—nice, friendly, and nurturing. Being successful means you are competitive, confident and forceful, not likeable. We are greatly conflicted between what we want to be: successful and powerful or nice and nurturing. People still believe it is impossible to combine both. Many times, in my career I was called the "Ice Queen".

Bottom line: We should all strive to work on eradicating this mind set and behavior of not owning up to our accomplishments. It is going to take work and support from both other women and men to overcome this socialization of decades.

> *"Believe in yourself and negotiate for yourself. Own your own success."*
>
> *-Sheryl Sandberg, COO Facebook, #5 on Forbes 100 Most Powerful Women List*

Change #2 Listen to your intuition.

Men are trained to make decisions based on empirical facts. They deride women who rely on emotions. But they are wrong, according to Dr. Kelly Turner who has studied intuition extensively.

"Studies have found that when it comes to making major life decisions such as which house to buy or which person marry, trusting your intuition leads to better outcomes than trusting your logical, thinking brain," she states.

A study of car buyers found that those who extensively researched their choice were satisfied only 25% of the time. By contrast, buyers who made a quick, intuitive decision were pleased 60% of the time.

Make a conscious effort to listen to your gut feeling. Much has been written and a lot said about "women's intuition." While it is simply not true that only women have "intuition", it is easy to see how that idea developed—as a put down. The association of reason with men and nature with women dates to the Greeks.

Aristotle defined man as a rational animal, and by that, he meant men specifically not human beings. He saw women as less able to reason, hence, less human and more animal. In Europe, well into the 20th century, women were generally seen as somehow "intellectually deficient."

An English woman recently became Oxford's oldest living graduate. Even though she had completed her degree courses in the 1920's, (but with a blatant show of chauvinism at that time,) Oxford did not award degrees to female students. Presumably it would have decreased the status of the university to award degrees to an "intellectually inferior sex."

Women's conversations often emphasize feelings, which may mean that we think about feelings more. It does not mean that we are more emotional. It is perfectly possible that men are just as emotional but for social reasons they talk and think less about their feelings.

The Cognitive Psychologists call it "learned expertise." What seems to be happening in our brains, studies reveal, is that the mind sorts information unconsciously and rapidly provides a conclusion. Research also shows that conscious practice improves our recognition of intuitive solutions. Firefighters rely on intuition to alert them to danger. Professional gamblers use it to win.

> *"Don't let other opinions drown out your inner voice, and most importantly, have the courage to follow your heart and intuition.*

> *They somehow already know what you truly*
> *want to become."*
>
> -Stephen Jobs, Inventor, Cofounder/CEO
> Apple Inc.

Change # 3 Network with purpose.

Many of us fall into a rut. But ruts limit our experiences and opportunities, therefore, resolve to "get your feet on the street" as we say in the sales business.

Networking does not mean just collecting business cards and filling your rolodex. It is about developing relationships.

Yes, this is the era of social media and networking can occur on line. Indeed, my daughter has used internet networking very effectively, and she met one of her top mentors on line. But nothing takes the place of face-to-face meetings.

So, if you want a new job or increased business, make sure you go to other organizations where you meet people. Be deliberate in choosing where you spend your time and how you spend your efforts. While a glass of wine (just one by the way) might be a pleasant respite after a hard day at the office, a free glass of wine is not the main reason you are going to this mixer.

> *"The richest people in the world*
> *Look for and build networks,*
> *Everyone else looks for work."*
>
> -Robert Kloyosaki,
> Author, Rich Man Poor Man

But it is more than just attending; it is actively participating, getting involved. Engage. Be present.

And then put your big girl panties on; stick your hand out; introduce yourself. Change your attitude and be assertive. Don't just stand there with your attentive, nice girl face on and let the men do all the pontificating. Like dieting or exercising, most of us know how to network, we just have to make it a priority.

I realize breaking into a small group you do not know is uncomfortable. Now you obviously must learn to be tactful; wait for the right moment; look for other newbies like yourself. But the more often you do this, the better you become at spotting times and groups of people who you can approach.

It simply is something we women must get better at. Men do this all the time and for years have been strong networkers. From prestigious schools to athletic clubs to dining clubs, men use their contacts productively in business.

> *"I think women are really good at making friends and not good at networking. Men are good at networking and not so good at making friends. That's a gross generalization, but I think it holds true in many ways."*
>
> -Madeleine Albright, Diplomat, First Female US Secretary of State

For many years when I was working, I thought my job was to get my work done as efficiently and as good as possible. I was incorrect. While of course there is an element of that, getting out there is essential to your long-term career.

I consider an event a success if I can pick up just one kernel of new information or meet one new person. Just think how that adds up.

When I was at GM, I met a woman at a function for the local advertising organization. It felt like there was a cast of thousands, lots of drinking and hail fellows well met, as was the custom in the raucous Detroit automotive business. I went up to the other woman in the room, stuck out my hand and said:

"Hi, I'm Chris Meyers."

"Oh, I really wanted to meet you," she said. I immediately felt important as I puffed up.

"Yeah, I hear you are as big a bitch, as I am," Karen Ritchie said. Most likely true.

Over the years, Karen I became fast friends. She became the highest-ranking woman in the automotive advertising business, as EVP of MediaWorks, the agency which placed hundreds of millions of dollars for GM in all media.

My two favorite rewards from reaching out to different women are:

First, you find out how much we are alike. That you are not alone…no matter how perfect, how beautiful, how together you think the woman next to you is…. she isn't. Everyone has lived through problems, and often much worse than yours.

> *"Nearly every glamorous, wealthy successful woman you might envy now, started out as some kind of schlepp."*
>
> *-Helen Gurley Brown, Transformed from "mouseburger" to legendary Editor of Cosmopolitan Magazine*

The second reward from reaching out is that you may be able to help another woman. Your experiences, your expertise may be able to lift up another woman, help her face her own fears.

You will find the opportunity to "pay it forward". I do believe that heroines are born and re-born every day as we face each obstacle in our everyday lives. We each can be THE ONE to someone. You never know where that someone might be.

In network marketing, you may think the reward is just money, but the relationships will far outweigh the money, and in the end, it will be all about the lives you change, including your own.

Change # 4 Tackle risk full on.

Get out of your rut. Do it and your horizons will expand to include places and experiences you may never have imagined existed.

I realize that taking a risk means moving out of your comfort zone. This means being more proactive with your life…and going out on a limb to control the events of your life. Author Nora Ephron calls it, "being the star of your own story, instead of a bit player".

By nature, women tend to be more risk adverse than men. There are obviously times when playing it safe is a good route—be careful who you meet at the hot singles bar, don't dive head first into an unfamiliar pool or lake, don't gossip about your new boss. But you can wear a sexy red thong and matching bra under that sober business suit. And revel in the way it dispels your feelings of drab old you. Victoria's Secret built a business on that insight.

In business and sometimes life, being risk adverse results in stagnation. Boredom. The cost of most stability is the curtailment of your growth.

But if you do nothing, you get nothing. So, there is, in a sense, a risk in not taking a risk. You settle. Playing it safe often means that you let life happen to you instead of for you. For me, it is better to say, "oops" than "what if."

When I look back on my life, my greatest rewards came when I when I took my greatest risks. After all, there are no "do overs" in life. Men and jobs come and go, but life, it only comes around once.

> "Life should not be a journey to the grave
> with the intention of arriving safely in a
> pretty and well preserved body, but rather to
> skid in broadside in a cloud of smoke,
> thoroughly used up, totally worn out, and
> loudly proclaiming "Wow!

-Hunter Thompson, Author, Founder Gonzo Journalism

You have just read some of my challenges with the ensuing changes and I hope, as you process them, you may learn how to better handle yours.

It is worth repeating that a change imposed is a change opposed. Do not let that imposition happen to you.

So here it is short and sweet. My suggestions for your guideposts:

Stop apologizing.

Listen to your intuition.

Network with purpose

Tackle risk.

We know that change happens, that we must anticipate change and adapt to it quickly. The quicker we let go of the old; the sooner we can enjoy the new.

So change. Enjoy the change. Savor the adventure. Then be ready to change quickly and enjoy it all over again.

***

To contact Chris:

Mobile: 252-269-4517

Email: chris.meyers.moore@hear-chris-speak.com

Web: www.hear-chris-speak.com

LinkedIn: linkedin.com/in/chris-meyers-moore

Web: www.eastern-carolina-economic-club.org

Email: chris@ecec-nc.org

Web: www.wellnesdirectory.com

Email: chris@wellnesdirectory.com (note one "s" in wellness)

Christie Garcia

Christie Garcia is a Leadership Coach, Speaker, Facilitator, and Founder of Mindful Choice.

Mindful Choice isn't just a name, it's a deep seeded ethos. It's a belief system for leadership development that's built around the core of an individual's self-awareness. A solution that leads to actions that are mindful of others, mindful of themselves, and mindful of the impact they have within an organization and the world around them. We offer solutions that empower leaders to transition out of the "I" mentality and begin to embrace the "We" in order to accomplish big- picture goals.

Christie's unique development approach has been changing the face of leadership in a broad spectrum of industries including startups, technology, distribution, global sales & manufacturing, human resources, hospitality, and construction.

Create Your Impact

By Christie Garcia

Dear Amazing, Awesome Reader,

Let's talk about *impact*. Not the impact of politics, or religion, or Aunt Betty's fruitcake. Yes, those all play a role in the world around us but I am talking about YOU and YOUR impact. I am curious about how you show up in every moment. Whether you are walking into a gas station or a conference room. Whether you are speaking with a five year-old or your boss.

I'm using the term *impact* as your overall effect on someone or something. It can be good or bad, it can also be strong or weak. We create an impact with our words, our body language, our expressions, and most importantly, the one that gets overlooked, *our energy*. I know, energy is a *'fluffy coach'* term but think of it as your physical and emotional mood. People feel this energy (your mood) without you having to say a single word.

So, ask yourself:

What is my impact?

Am I getting the results I want out of life, relationships, communication, work, etc.?

Truth be told, most people think *their impact is better than it really is*, or, *they don't realize how good their impact is*. Neither perspective is wrong; this simply means that most people live their whole life without knowing their true impact. I personally believe this is a sad reality for humanity. I know that sounds dramatic but think about it; if **you don't know how good your impact** is then you never truly own your greatness so you are unable to give your natural gifts away to family, friends, or your community. The opposite side of this is, if **you think your impact is better than it**

really is then you lose the opportunity to truly maximize your potential which leads to the same problem; the world will never truly benefit and learn from your true gifts. Instead, your mistakes will serve as a lesson of what not to do.

After years of working with many different businesses, and with people of all ages at every career level, I've realized impact is a concept that many of us never stop to think about. We simply '*do what we do*' and hope for the best.

I am a big believer that ***our impact is the one thing we can control*** in this world. We can't change how people *perceive* us but we can change our approach, our language, and our energy to improve how people *react* to us. It's kind of like the theory that kindness is contagious. If you treat people with kindness you will encourage others to be kind. When you improve your impact you will naturally encourage others to improve theirs.

So, here it is, the simple formula to maximize your impact today!

MINDFULNESS

(The art of being conscious of ourselves and the world around us.)

+

SELF-AWARENESS

(Why we do what we do, why we feel what we feel, and how we show up in good, bad and ugly times.)

=

CREATING YOUR IMPACT

(The ability to intentionally create an outcome through your words, thoughts, feelings, actions, and energy.)

IMPACT is the one thing that can directly change the world around us; *if we are all willing to improve it*. It is single handedly our biggest super power. We can choose a happy, positive approach or the negative, downer approach. We can encourage and develop people or we can compete and dictate. We can shy away from our truth and please others or we can speak our truth and learn to work through tough conversations. We can be the person who creates and encourages fun or we can be the fun killer. Get the picture? We all know someone who falls into each of these categories. We are usually pretty good at picking out who falls where. The part we aren't always good at is figuring out where we fall ourselves. This is due to not being mindful, which creates a lack of self-awareness that results in **unintentional impact.**

Good news for you, all of this is about to change! You are going to get a crash course on being more mindful and self-aware, so ***you can improve your OWN impact*** with every interaction.

STEP ONE: BECOMING MINDFUL

Creating choice and taking back YOUR control.

My company is called Mindful Choice because I believe that when we are mindful of our self and the world around us we have choice. **Choice gives us power**. When choice is taken away from us we feel *powerless*. Everything around us seems *chaotic*. We begin to *surrender*. Eventually we are just going through the motions of life trying to survive. Sometimes we think about what we are doing and sometimes we just do something to scratch it off of our list so we can get on to the next thing. Sound familiar?

What if I told you that you could buy more time, you could have more productive conversations, and you could eliminate the daily problem-solve roller coaster ride? Would you believe me if I told you that you could stop feeling overwhelmed and anxious when one more thing is added to your to-do list? Well, you can! All you have to do is be a little more mindful throughout your day.

We are all busy, so I can assure you that becoming mindful is not about adding things to your schedule, or removing important things from your schedule, or telling you to start doing yoga or meditating regularly. It just means that you *slow down (or stop)* and get curious.

*Curiosity i*s the key to being mindful in the current moment. When we feel overwhelmed and are just going through the motions we get tunnel vision. We do things the way they've always been done, how we were taught, or maybe we've just gotten lazy and we rely on what is '*normal'*.

The next time you start to feel this way, stop. Ask yourself the following questions:

>   *Why am I doing _____?*
>   *Why does _____ matter?*

These two questions may be all you need to realize you are doing things throughout your day that just don't matter. We create so many extra tasks, issues, and unnecessary circumstances because we think we are supposed to. Maybe someone said, "*we should be doing this*", or "*our friends are all doing this*", or worse yet, social media says, "*We're a bad (parent, spouse, friend, employee, boss, etc.) if you don't*".

If you *just recognized* the voice in your head that makes you say, "yes" to things because you are afraid of being judged or not wanting to disappoint others, *congratulations!* You just identified your first saboteur (the little voice that sabotages your life). By identifying this saboteur, you just bought yourself time, control and most importantly, sanity. Here comes the fun part…go through every task that overwhelms you and ask yourself why are you doing it and does it matter? Saboteurs can create some pretty powerful reasons to why we need to do something so make sure you *dig deep and find the real purpose*. Then you can decide if it's really worth it.

Now, I'm sure there are several of you who didn't quite get all you needed from those first two questions, so let's take it a step further.

Why does it matter to you?

Why does it matter to others?

(Think about all parties involved - family, community, companies, clients, peers, friends, the earth, etc...)

Will it matter in five days, six months, or two years from now?

The further your answers get from being **about you**, the more mindful you become to the real issue at hand. You see *more options*, which will *create choice*. **Choice creates power**. When we have power we loosen our grip on life because *we trust we are okay*. When we don't have choice we feel *trapped*. We feel *powerless*. Our **mind spins** and we start adding more fillers into our days and schedules just *to feel like we have control over something*.

It's **exhausting and stressful** just thinking about how we do this.

STOP the madness and identify where you have lost your power! Ask the questions above, over and over, until you figure out where you have *forfeited your control* and *why you gave it up*. Most of the time we don't realize we've lost control, life just happens and usually the feeling of chaos is the symptom that forces us to reassess.

Deep breath in...and exhale!

Now that you know how to be mindful let's move on to step two.

STEP TWO: BECOMING SELF-AWARE

Own your thoughts, emotions and actions.

Self-awareness is the simple trick to happiness. In order to create your own happiness, you must be willing to understand why you do what you do, why you feel what you feel, and how you show up at your best and worst. If you *know yourself inside and out*, then no person or circumstance can take you down or own your emotions. You must always remember that if you don't control your own thoughts and emotions then someone or something else will. ***Self-***

awareness is the only tool that allows you to control your own mind.

I will warn you, *as a person who preaches and practices self-awareness daily*, this is a life-long study that cannot be mastered. The sooner you embrace your good, your bad and your ugly the easier life and all of its challenges will be.

So, here are some steps to help you get started!

First, **you must be honest with yourself.** You are the only one who can wake up and go to bed knowing your truth so you must hold yourself to your highest integrity. Don't put on a show. It's *you*, just *yourself.* Don't be mean or deny the side of you that is not perfect. You are your own worst critic; you must *stop judging yourself* and *start embracing all of YOU* (even the ugly side).

Second, **our strengths are the same as our weaknesses**. When we over use our strength it eventually holds us back. For example, if you are a kind person that is a huge strength. If you are kind and don't create boundaries, then you can be taken advantage of. If you are direct and speak truth you are courageous. If you are too direct without a relatable tone, then you can be a jerk. If you are confident you can lead people. If you are too confident you can be mistaken as arrogant. If you are able to empathize with others, you are caring and thoughtful. If you are too empathetic you take on others issues and make them your own. This is the best part of self-awareness. **It's your good and bad.** You can't have one without the other so **OWN IT!**

In a moment, I am going to ask you to **stop judging yourself and get real**. To help you do this I want to share *two types of self-judgment* that hold you back from your truth. The person who **beats themselves up with negativity** and the person who **raises themselves up with praise**. While you reflect pay attention to whether or not it is easier to identify with your strengths or your weaknesses.

If it is easier to find your strengths, then most likely you struggle with feedback and criticism. The only way to overcome this is by owning your weaknesses. If you know you are confident, you must learn when does it turn to arrogance. If you are competitive, you need to know when the competition isn't *fun* for others.

If it's easier for you to find your weaknesses, then you are probably a person who seeks validation from others and you need to start identifying your own greatness and self-worth. List all of your amazing gifts so you can see that your weaknesses are great too. *We cannot have a strength without a weakness* so have fun and create your list of good, bad, and ugly!

This is YOU, celebrate it!

So here it is, the **Self-awareness Challenge**: I dare you to stop for five minutes and get real! Here are some questions to help you become more mindful of yourself and the life you are living.

> *Who are you?*
>
> *What do you want out of life?*
>
> *What makes you happy? Sad? Angry?*
>
> *Who brings the BEST out in you? What does your best look like? How does it feel?*
>
> *Who brings the WORST out in you? What does your worst look like? How does it feel?*
>
> *What are your core values?*

(These are the things you can't live without. Our emotions are tightly connected to our values and belief systems. Think about what makes you happiest and the most upset - your values are most likely being honored or stepped on.)

> *What are your top 10 strengths and weaknesses?*

These questions can go on forever. **Stay curious and check-in daily** by setting reminders in your phone or putting post-it notes on your fridge or computer.

Alright, now that you're on the path to becoming more *mindful and self-aware* let's move onto step three to find out how it all relates to impact.

STEP THREE: CREATE YOUR IMPACT

Mindfulness + Self-awareness allows you to *intentionally* show up in the world.

Remember when I told you that you could buy more time, have more productive conversations, eliminate the daily roller coaster ride, and stop feeling so overwhelmed and anxious when one more thing is added to your to-do list? **This is the secret!** By combining mindfulness and self-awareness you control your time, your emotions, and *you get to show up in a powerful and effective way!*

Here's what this can look like:

Sean is an easy-going guy that doesn't like to rock the boat. For the last several months he has attended a weekly meeting with his team. He doesn't love the direction the project is going but he doesn't want to be the negative guy so he finds it easier to just say "okay" and agree with the plan. Each week he leaves frustrated and upset. He tends to vent to people who weren't in the meetings to get their opinions which usually frustrates him even more. Finally, something happens in the next meeting that he can't say, "okay" to anymore. He throws up his hands, digs in his heels and *stops agreeing*. There is confusion in the room because this is the first time in months he refused the plan. On top of that, the message was emotionally driven due to the several months of frustration and buildup. The team members are confused so they start to get a bit defensive. Voices start to raise and all of sudden the peaceful meeting turned into chaos.

I'm sure most of you are shaking your head because you have been in a similar situation. Maybe you were Sean or maybe you were a member on his team. This is an example of '*unintentional impact*'. The good news is there is a better way. You just have to be mindful and self-aware so you can create the impact you want.

If Sean recognized that his strength of being agreeable and '*going along to get along*' has the built-in weakness of *passive-aggressive, emotional explosions* he could have reduced the chance of that chaos from ever happening. Imagine all of those months of worry and drama that he created after each meeting. On top of that, Sean's explosion *implied* the work of the rest of the team was *irrelevant*. If Sean had stopped long enough to clarify what he was frustrated with and trusted himself to communicate his thoughts from the beginning his impact would have been more productive. He also would not have been **wasting his own time and everyone else's.**

Now, I'm not saying that being mindful and self-aware will make all life's problems go away. I'm saying it will **shift your perspective** to allow you to see a better way. This **helps you create options**. The option to have the *courage and confidence to speak up* when needed; or to *change your language when you are speaking your truth* and it is not being heard. It will also prevent you from saying "yes" to tasks or ideas when you realize that you have the option to say "no".

Here are a couple of questions that can help you intentionally create your impact.

What is the outcome I want?

(Consider the task, the feelings, and the facts)

How do I need to show up to achieve that outcome?

(This includes, your energy, vocal tones, body language, emotions, and facial expressions.)

What are my emotional triggers for this topic? Why?

(A trigger creates an emotional response. Ex: disrespect could be the underlying trigger for road rage.)

What is the perspective and feelings of the person you are speaking to?

(Why does it matter to others involved? What are the facts? How do you achieve the best results?)

Your impact is your **super power**; it's your choice to own it and use it.

Well, **you did it**! You made it to the end of this chapter and I'm confident you are already more aware and mindful than you were five minutes ago. Continue to build these skills and you will improve your impact and take back the control of your life.

Stay **MINDFUL**. Get curious and reconnect to your bigger life. What are you worrying about today that won't matter in five days? Six months? Or ten years from now?

Be **SELF-AWARE**. You are on this planet at this time in history so don't waste it by judging yourself, worrying about what others think, or doing things that just exhaust you. *Slow down and be mindful* of why you do what you do. **This is you - own it and celebrate all of you!**

Always **CREATE YOUR IMPACT**. Speak your truth, hold onto your integrity, and be your best self! You have an impact whether you want it or not. You may as well own it and mindfully create it. That is the only way to build a world that fills you up versus wears you out.

So, go on, I dare you to take charge of your life!

Mindfully Yours,

Christie

P.S. If you want more tips and tricks send me a message. I'd love to hear from you!

***

To Contact Christie:

Phone: 415-971-9535

Email: info@mindfulchoicecoaching.com

www.mindfulchoicecoaching.com

www.facebook.com/mindfulchoice

*Visit this website for **your free gift:***
www.mindfulchoicecoaching.com/gift

Use Promo Code: TheChange

Anthony G. Solimini Jr.

Anthony Solimini is a seasoned banker, sales professional, sales coach, public speaker, motivator, and trainer (and also a stand-up comedian!) who transforms average salespeople, negotiators, and leaders into rock stars.

A proud Bostonian, he has worn many hats in his 26 years of professional experience in London, Singapore, Bangkok, and Hong Kong with such companies as JP Morgan, Lenovo, Heineken, Societe Generale, Deutsche Bank, Gulf Oil, Freshfields, the US Consulate, Morgan Stanley, and Bank of America. He is fully certified in the Sandler Sales Process and The Management Group's Leadership 360 program.

One thing Anthony knows for certain is that what separates winners from "averagers" is their ability to communicate effectively, charismatically, and passionately. So in his coaching and training work with individuals and groups, he empowers people to master body language, humor, "power" words, and confidence so they become more charismatic, compelling, effective, and inspiring. And successful!

A published author of two books, Anthony is a self-confessed travel junkie, having visited 41 countries! He is happily married, currently lives in Hong Kong, and spends as much time as possible at his home in Marco Island, Florida.

How M&M's Changed My Life

By Anthony Solimini Jr.

I can honestly say that I've always felt blessed. Always! My entire life, things have just seemed to fall into place, one after the other, and now, somehow, at 54 years of age, I find myself living in Hong Kong with an amazing wife, good health, and financial security, with real estate investments in Florida, where we plan to retire.

So how does a person from a middle-class family go from a small town in Boston to global citizen, with jobs in financial services in London, Singapore, Thailand and Hong Kong?

The story starts when I was a child. I was the youngest of four in an Italian-American family. My parents, specifically my father, were always telling us we could be anything we wanted to be, and that nothing could stop us. But for me, I knew there was more to it. I knew there was a lot to learn and a lot to do if I was to become as successful as I could be.

And that's where M&M's come in. No, not the candies (although they *have* been a huge part of my life!). No, what I mean is MONITORING and MODELING.

Let me give you an example. My dad, like many Italian-Americans, was of course a huge Frank Sinatra fan. Huge. As I was growing up, the smooth voice of Ol' Blue Eyes played constantly throughout our house. I remember my dad singing along with Frank, and I noticed that over the years dad's voice got better, and better, and better. By the time I was in college, it seemed that my dad's voice was almost identical to that of "the Chairman of the Board." And at a young age it occurred to me that my dad was simply using an EXPERT in his field to learn how to sing like him. He did that with the piano too. With no formal training, my dad could play the piano like a concert pianist. How? Well, he played records (yes, vinyl) of famous pianists that he enjoyed, and slowly started striking the keys in such a way that it all came together and he was able to play like an expert. Again, he MONITORED the experts and MODELED himself on them.

That's what I mean by M&M's. My dad was, in essence, RECREATING excellence. Why re-invent the wheel? If you love Sinatra's voice, study it, listen to it, observe it, and then try and recreate it. If you love golf, watch the best golfers in the world. Pretty soon you can start modeling your swing after theirs, and voilà, you're shooting better scores.

See, my dad taught me: Never, ever, accept anything but the best. Never, ever, assume you can't do something. His favorite quote was "It's not what you think you are, it's what you *think*, you *are*." There's a HUGE difference. So from a young age, I just assumed I'd be successful. I had zero doubt. I learned from my dad that if someone can do something, *anyone* should be able to do it. And that's how my journey started.

Let me take you back to my high-school years. I went to an all-boys Catholic high school where there were two groups of students: The A group and the B group. I was in the B group, which meant my grades and qualifications weren't as good as those of the students in the A group. And of course the A group got better teachers, better classes, and more interesting topics. So what did I do? I monitored and modeled the behaviors and activities of the A group. What did *they* do that I didn't? Well, for one thing, they studied. And for another, they were always doing extra-curricular activities: sports, theater, volunteering, the school newspaper, AV club… So I started hanging around the A group more and more. I started playing sports, and did theater and as many extracurricular activities as possible. Finally, because math was my favorite subject, I approached the head of the math department and told him I wanted to push myself and learn more about the subject. And guess what? He put me in the

A group for math. My grades dropped, but it helped me in the next phase of my life: college.

When I was 17 and looking for colleges to apply to, I was once again blessed. My best friend from childhood, who was a year older than me, attended Creighton University in Omaha, Nebraska, and told me to consider it. Now you might be wondering why someone from Boston, with some of the best universities in the world, would want to go to Omaha, Nebraska. Well, once again, it's because I believed in MONITORING and MODELING.

So I asked myself: Why not go to a different part of the USA, interact with people from different backgrounds and see where it takes me? That turned out to be another amazing learning experience. Surrounded by smart, interesting, culturally diverse people from all over the USA and other parts of the world, I was able to add even more behaviors to my database of "success." I was able to MODEL myself on them, combining all of the best traits I'd observed over my short lifetime. For example, I noticed that the fraternities were full of confident, smart, charismatic students. So of course I joined a fraternity, Pi Kappa Alpha. The people I met, the skills I learned, and the role models I found enabled me to rise to another level at college.

Please understand that MODELING is *not* copying. In fact, it's the exact opposite – it's about achieving a desired outcome by monitoring and studying how someone else goes about it. One summer during college, I worked as a waiter in a five-star restaurant in Boston, MA. Most summer staff did their jobs just to earn some money. Not me. I was at a five-star restaurant in a city filled with very wealthy people, so I spent the summer learning about wine by observing and monitoring what wine connoisseurs bought. What they talked about. What they did to the wine before they drank it. I asked questions. I told them I wanted to learn. And guess what: by the end of the summer, I'd learned more than any course or training session could have provided.

Insights into Self-Empowerment

By the time I was 22, my instinct of monitoring and modeling had paid off. I was convinced that with the right amount of confidence and a basic understanding of how certain behaviors trigger certain outcomes, I was in for a successful life. It just so happened that I was born with this instinct, but I can share with you how you can get this instinct for yourself and be more confident and successful!

Many things need to be aligned for you to be successful, but most significant among them are your beliefs and your attitude! You have to be passionate about succeeding and achieving what you want to achieve. You have to believe you can do it, and that you *will* do it. But it won't be easy! I heard a great comment by the world-ranked MMA fighter, Connor McGregor. He was told how lucky he was to have achieved so much success in such a short amount of time, and he responded:

"There's no talent here, this is hard work. This is an obsession. Talent does not exist; we are all equal as human beings. You could be anyone if you put in the time. You will reach the top, and that is that. I am not talented, I am obsessed."

I love his comment "we are all equal". That's the truth! When I wanted to leave the USA and move overseas for international work opportunities, I talked and worked with people who'd already done it. *They* had done it, so why couldn't I? What did they do? Why were they successful? What made *them* get the opportunities and not other people? I ALWAYS believed that I could do whatever I wanted to if I committed to something. So first and foremost, believe in yourself, believe in the power of adapting your behaviors, and have the confidence to go for it without worrying about failure! Get rid of all your self-limiting beliefs and learn the power of "I can do anything."

Another thing I learned on my journey to success was about "positive" vs "negative" thinking. It sounds so simple, but most people approach life from a negative mindset, meaning they focus on what they *don't* want to happen rather than what they *do* want to happen. For me, I always knew what type of life I wanted, what type of job I wanted and what type of wife I wanted to spend the rest of my life with. I was totally focused: I could see, feel and taste those successes in my mind. It was like I'd created a movie when I was young, and directed my way to success. Sure, life can be hard and things don't always go according to plan, but that's the beauty of it. The more we do, the more we learn and the better chance we have of success.

Rid your mind of negative thoughts. Let go of friends and family members who drain you of your positive energy. Surround yourself with people who make you want to get up in the morning and be the best you can be. Create a Mastermind Group and meet every week, share best practices, help each other, and learn as much as you can from successful people! When I started my first company in 2003, I did just that. I had to "divorce" many of my friends and family who didn't have the same passion and ambitions as I did. I had to rid myself of doubters who questioned my decision to start my own business. They asked me how I could leave the comfort and security of a banking job to enter the world of the unknown. But that was a long time ago – now, most of my friends and colleagues have a positive mindset! We all believe we can do whatever we want to if we monitor and model ourselves after people who've been there before us.

In my first book, I talked about the power of TRUST, COMFORT and CONFIDENCE, and how you need to master all three elements in order to succeed. I wrote it from a sales perspective, but it applies to life as well. Our interactions with people determine our success, so if you can't communicate and adapt to different situations and ways of thinking, you'll fail.

So we start with TRUST. Why? Without trust you can't move any relationship forward. If the people you want to work with, socialize with, partner with, and learn with don't trust you, they won't help you! And in order to monitor and model certain behaviors, you need access to people who trust you and are willing to share with you. So how do you become a more trustworthy person? It's very simple: Be honest, sincere, and dedicated to whatever it is you're trying to achieve. Stay calm, reciprocate where appropriate, always tell the truth, and never go back on your word.

You also need to get inside the minds of others, which brings me to the next element: COMFORT. Have you ever been to a function and met someone, and for some reason you clicked? It's as if you've been friends for years. When that happens, you end up talking more openly and honestly with that person. Conversely, if you don't click with someone, you put up your defense mechanisms and want to get away as soon as possible. So you need to make people feel comfortable. Make them want to be around you. Make them want to help you. And one way to do that is to adapt your communication style to the person you're speaking to. This helps create a stronger sense of rapport or connection, and helps people to understand you.

We all see the world in different ways. If I'm a very analytical, detail-oriented person and someone tries to communicate with me with a high-level, big-picture strategy, there's a major disconnect. Communication stops. Remember, if the person you're communicating with doesn't understand you, it's not their fault, it's yours. So without charismatic, powerful, clear, concise, empathetic communication skills, everything can come tumbling down. Watch videos of speakers you admire, learn from them, and commit to speaking in public as much as you can. Don't be shy. All great leaders and successful businesspeople are amazing communicators!

Finally, we come to the third element that, for me, separates the winners from the losers, the successful from the unsuccessful: CONFIDENCE. You need to exhibit confidence in yourself and your goals. You need to believe that you're invincible and can do anything. Without this, you won't be able to reach your full potential. You'll hesitate, and you'll lack the courage and conviction to keep moving forward. Everyone around you can see how you feel about yourself, and you can't hide insecurity.

You can't hide confidence either – people see it, and they want to be around you. But don't confuse this with arrogance. Confidence is simply the belief that if you work hard, learn from others, and apply new behaviors, you *will* succeed.

Let me give you an example. In 2010 I was consulting for a major financial institution and led some training for the new graduate trainees – 30 young men and women all armed with an MBA and a 4.0 GPA. So in a sense, all equal. For the next two years they were going to be put through an intensive and fun program, at the end of which they'd get a new role inside the organization. Within the first two weeks of training and coaching these young men and women, I knew who would get a *great* job and who would get a merely "average" job. I could do this with 100% accuracy. How? Simply by observing their communication skills, confidence, body language, attire, commitment to the workload, commitment to asking challenging questions, and, of course, willingness to take on the role of a leader in the class. Yet they all had an MBA and a 4.0 GPA from a top university. Trust, comfort and confidence are the fuel that can take you and your business to a whole new level.

So when I talk about monitoring and modeling, what I really mean is that typically, confident, successful people know that success is not the goal, it's the *result*. What's the goal? To learn, observe and educate yourself as much as you can about your chosen field of interest.

In my case, I graduated from Creighton University with a 2.7 GPA in Mathematics and Computer Science. Now as you may know, a 2.7 is not exactly top of the class. It's average at best! Yet I managed to apply to, and get *into*, the Boston University School of Dentistry, one of the top dental schools in the country. How? Well, I was told it was because of my interview. I met with a board member of the school as part of the application process, and we absolutely hit it off. I didn't feel threatened by her, even though she was a very successful dental professor and had the power to admit me or reject me. But I was honest, sincere, and confident about my abilities, so I told her about my strengths and the areas where I knew I needed to improve.

At that point, I noticed a math book on her book shelf. Now I had zero knowledge of dentistry, but I had just graduated with a degree in Mathematics and Computer Science. So as a confident, positive person I asked her about the book. Sure enough, she was taking some math courses at the university and asked whether we could have a chat about what she was studying. The next 90 minutes pretty much sold her on my abilities and confidence, and I was accepted into a class of 30 students, from a field of over 4,000 applicants. And to top it all off, I went on to become president of the freshman class. All that with a 2.7 GPA!

I have many stories like that, but let me end by offering you a list of what I think are the skills and traits that separate the successful from the unsuccessful. They've definitely helped me on my 54-year journey to success.

1. Understand that confidence comes from experience and knowledge.
2. Know what you want to achieve.
3. Take action.
4. Stay away from negative people and thoughts.
5. Learn to communicate like a rock star, with everyone from the janitor to the CEO.
6. Always help others to achieve their goals.
7. Ask for help when you need it.
8. Be well groomed at all times.
9. Smile and laugh as much as possible.
10. Be prepared for success and good fortune to come your way.

Good luck, and always remember the inspiring words of Walt Disney:

"Somehow I can't believe that there are any heights that can't be scaled by a man who knows the secrets of making dreams come true. This special secret, it seems to me, can be summarized in four Cs: curiosity, confidence, courage, and constancy, and the greatest of all is confidence. When you believe in a thing, believe in it all the way, implicitly and unquestionably."

***

To contact Anthony:

ags@anthonysolimini.com

+865 9306 7865 (Hong Kong)

Website: www.anthonysolimini.com

Bernie Garrett

Bernie Garrett was born 10th in a family of thirteen children, and decided early if he was to stand out in the crowd, he had to be different than the rest.

His Mother often said to him, "If you are going to say something, make it worthwhile, otherwise you are just another voice in the crowd." She still can't believe people pay him for what she told him to stop doing many times as a kid.

A devoted husband, father and grandfather, Bernie's passion is people and adding value to their life, so when he returned home from living and working in China for almost ten years, he focused on building a reputation of professional service and client appreciation.

Today, Bernie focuses on developing your 'Self-Leadership' and professional sales skills within organizations, businesses, teams and individuals through his leadership principles and making a difference in their business and personal lives.

His dream is to become a professional Motivational Speaker.

His Mission is to have a positive influence in people's lives.

His Vision is to add value to leaders who can multiply value to many.

His Passion is people, and helping them uncover their true potential in life.

Armed for Success

By Bernie Garrett

Failure is not the opposite of Success it's part of Success.

"It's only money, and if I can earn that much once, I can certainly make the same amount again." These were the words coming out of my mouth as I sat on the edge of the bed, tears streaming down my face, looking at my wife curled up, hiding from the world, not knowing how we were going to face the rest of our lives.

The year was 2006, and we were coming to the end of our ten-year expatriate life, working and living in China, when at the cusp or returning home to Australia, our investments and life savings had been embezzled by an international money scam organization. How was I going to overcome this situation and find the direction I now needed to go in?

In 1996 I celebrated my thirty-fourth birthday, I had been married for thirteen years, had three beautiful children and now on my way to Orlando Florida, to be recognized for the success in sales within the company I worked for in Australia, and to attend an international sales achiever's conference in America.

I had been working for this company for almost six years, and as a result of this trip, I was offered a job to move to Shanghai China in late 1996. My role was to coach, lead and mentor this new and vibrant sales team as the Regional Sales Manager-Eastern China.

My wife Ruth asked me at the time why I needed to work overseas and not stay in Australia, and I said, "I have something to offer," but wasn't sure exactly what it was, but I knew I couldn't scratch that itch if I stayed in Australia.

Coming from a large family, my mother would often say, "touch a heart, and they will give you their hand." My father would often say, "opportunities come when you are prepared for them." I took that advice from a young age and built my success based on hard work and integrity.

Ruth and I discussed moving to China over several weeks and decided to take up the companies offer and move to China. Little did I know that this opportunity was to set in motion, changes that would ultimately touch our lives forever.

We relocated to Shanghai during Chinese New Year in 1997. We had only accepted a three-year 'stay', which would be negotiated at the end of that period whether the company wanted me to remain any longer, based on my success and results.

Over the coming months, I fell right into my work, as my two daughters, Jessica 9years and Laura 6years, went back to school. Our youngest son (Callan) had not yet started pre-school but was only a couple of months away from commencing. Ruth, on the other hand, was coming to terms with living in China, trying to communicate and understand a new culture and way of life.

In those early months, Ruth would ask me, "what are we doing here?" and I would always say, "I have something to offer this company and the team around me." She would ask me, "how can you manage so many people when you have only ever managed a couple of people back in Australia?"

I didn't know it at the time, but I was developing a process called ARMED, that would become part of my success journey in China and subsequently, is still used today in how I run my business and live my life.

The sales team wanted success, and they wanted to feel that success, because that was a vision they saw of other western companies, and by association, they believed success was inevitable.

The key to success is a positive attitude.

The 'A' in ARMED stands for Attitude. Some of the sales team and area managers weren't all that excited about having to listen to a foreigner tell them how to become a success in their own country. What they did not realize at the time, I was to have a significant impact in their lives, and for some, for many years to come.

My attitude to people has never changed since I was a child. It was and still is upbeat, optimistic and positive. Because of that, it has always been easy for me to connect with people and make them feel relaxed and appreciated. That was my approach to every individual within the organization.

You attract into your life who you are, not what you want, so for me to attract optimistic, positive salesclerks, I had to represent that persona twenty-four hours a day, seven days a week. It wasn't difficult because I had made the decision many years earlier to be positive and optimistic every day of my life. And besides, the results far exceed anyone's imaginations over a pessimistic approach to life.

As the years passed, so did my position and leadership influence within the organization, not only in China but the Asia Pacific region. People felt more optimistic because I was working with them and my positive attitude was having an effect on them as well.

Success is your duty, obligation, and responsibility.

The 'R' in ARMED stands for Responsibility. My role and responsibility was to build a dynamic sales team, while their role and responsibilities was to deliver against the sales targets.

When people don't share and communicate in an open and inviting environment, confusion reigns and objectives are not often met.

The more responsibility I took on as a leader within the organization, the more responsibility the sales team wanted me to give them. They felt empowered to do more and deliver more, as they believed and felt I would be there to support them and move them towards their success. Responsibility for most decisions in life is a choice we make based on beliefs and values.

Without taking responsibility, we dwell on life not changing.

Greater responsibility was bestowed upon me, as the success of the organization grew in China, so other markets wanted to know how they could also increase their success growth by having me involved in their organizations.

You plus Motivation equal success.

The 'M' in ARMED stands for Motivation. My motivation in China and Asia Pacific was to become successful in the eyes of the company, but for me to feel successful in what I was achieving.

I soon realized I could not motivate another person because motivation is an emotion that comes from within all of us. I could, however, inspire people to do more than they thought possible. If I could identify that desire for the sales team to achieve more, they in-turn would be motivated to deliver more.

My travelling increased, and my level of self-motivation seemed to increase, the more success we enjoyed as a company. Influencing the various sales organizations on how to build successful sales teams, and how to build a great relationship with customers all over the world, increased the motivation levels of different sales teams in the regions.

Your Energy will build your success.

The 'E' in ARMED stands for Energy. Most people turn up to an event, to dinner or even to work, but that's as far as their energy levels allow them. They just turn-up. Their body is there, but they don't seem to want to engage, communicate or participate.

The salesclerks were often asked by our competitors in the market, how our company was growing so fast, when products and solutions were often very similar. When I reflect on this comment, it always brings a smile to my face, because our salesclerks had more energy than any other competitor in the market combined. Energy was a major contributor to the growth of the company, and every salesclerk new it.

Energy builds success, and positive energy attracts more positive energy. Don't just turn-up, 'show-up' to everything in life. When you show-up, your energy levels are heightened, your communication skills increase, and people want to engage with you. People can feel the energy in a room, a conversation and even when you are offering solutions to customers, they feel confident in your ability and your recommendations.

The secret of success is found in your daily habits.

The 'D' in ARMED stands for Daily Habits. This is the most important part of being ARMED for success. Without the development and the discipline of your daily habits, you will fail to reach your goals or objectives in business and in life. As John Maxwell said, "You will never change your life until you change what you do daily."

The salesclerks and the organization celebrated continuous success for almost ten years, and we built a team that was focused and inspired to achieve on a daily basis. We had built into their daily routines the needs and requirement for them to achieve small wins every day, thus giving them a sense of achievement and recognition every day.

When we celebrate daily goals achievements, we want to repeat that feeling in our mind and body, so it perpetuates again and again until we are disciplined every day to achieve our daily habits.

Success is measured by my personal happiness.

I soon realized in my journey in Asia, that success wasn't what I was achieving, but how I was feeling. My contract was coming to an end, while at the same time, my eldest daughter was leaving China and returning to Australia for University.

As a family, we were getting restless, and it was time to look at moving on or moving home. I quickly came to realize that I had done exactly what was expected of me for the past ten years. I had done my job, and I had delivered everything I had to offer. I had developed the 'armed' program that could be used by anyone, anywhere at any time, but would people understand the importance of it after I was gone.

The school year was ending in the coming June, so we made plans to relocate and repatriate back to Australia at the same time.

Success is achieved by using our strengths.

It was now the middle of June, and we were getting ready to relocate home. The kids had finished school, and we were ready to start again in Australia. Ruth and I had traveled back in May to secure schools and look for a new home, and now we were back in Beijing preparing for our repatriation.

I had been successful in my ten-year career living and working in China, and it was time to reap the rewards. We were home on this Friday when reading my emails, one, in particular, caused me some distress.

It was about the investment company that was looking after our money when an email warning mentioning the companies name appeared in my inbox.

I immediately felt sick and tried to call the company. No response, no answer. I tried every way I knew how to contact this company, but to no avail. I then rang the FBI in America.

Every muscle in my body was tense, and I had no idea what to say, but I rang anyway. I explained to them the events leading up to this moment and faxed and emailed all correspondence I had in procession to the FBI office. I was waiting for a callback, which seemed to take for hours.

The phone rang, and it was the FBI. They calmly asked me to repeat my story and all events leading up to this moment and explained to me that all our savings and investments had been embezzled and stolen by an international money scam organization. They asked me how much money was involved. It was a substantial seven figure amount in Australian dollars.

The FBI informed me that there was little or no chance to recover any funds and that the investigation could take years to uncover anything. I basically had to write the money off. This was devastating news and made even more so by having to tell Ruth we had lost everything we had been working towards?

Everything seemed to get worse the more I tried to explain. Not only had she warned me that she was never comfortable with the investment scheme, but that I seemed to ignore her wishes and proceeded to do what I thought best.

Three days of talking and crying and worrying never changed a thing.

"It's only money, and if I can earn that much once, I can certainly make the same amount again." This adage was running through my head, and it wasn't what Ruth wanted to here.

This was now the following Monday morning, and we were both exhausted. I put both feet on the ground as I got out of bed and decided I would start again.

It doesn't matter what happens to you in life; it's what happens within you that matters.

My analogy of success was completely wrong. I was under the impression that success was how high you climbed and how much money you could earn if you worked hard enough you could make a difference.

I then realized as I sat there, success is an emotional state of mind. Success is dependent on my personal growth, not my personal wealth. But now, in the eyes of Ruth I had failed at the one thing she was relying on for her future and the future of our family. I had taken away our family security.

This was just weeks before we relocated home to Australia and the thought of losing everything was overwhelming for both of us, but I was determined to bring that success back into my life.

As I sat there that Monday morning, and even as I reflect upon it now, I know I ARMED myself for the future with the five main areas of my life that I had complete control over.

My '<u>attitude</u>' never changed, because I knew my optimism and positive thought process I followed every day, would allow me to keep going. Now more than ever, I had to develop a greater level of positive emotional strength than ever before. I found new mentors to read about, listen to and reflect upon. This was the beginning of a brand new journey.

Now having to take '<u>responsibility</u>' for what had happened, and even more importantly, take responsibility for what I had to do now was at the forefront of my thoughts and actions. I had a duty and responsibility to rebuild my family's wealth security, and through this, my responsibility was to be accountable for my actions and future development.

'<u>Motivation</u>' has never been an issue for me, and it wasn't going to be impeded now. My motivation is driven by my imagination because that allows me to see a vision of what I want and need to create in my life. I am not going to say that this situation hadn't affected me because it had, but I knew I had to be stronger than the situation. I started to imagine what I could do when we moved back to Australia. I began to imagine how I could generate a new career or new wealth solution and the more I imagined the possibilities, the more inspired I became. I knew I had to move on and build something new in our life.

My 'energy' has always been and will always be on a high level, and now applying high energy into this situation, tested me more that I had ever been tested in my life. If I didn't focus my energy levels where they were most needed, my communication skills would have been affected, along with my body language and expectations. I needed to reflect my energy level because I needed to attract those people into my life now and into the future.

The one thing that I did change and refocus on was my 'daily habits'. These new habits had to focus on the small changes I needed to do every day that would move me in the direction of realizing my new goals. What I listened to, who I associated with, what I read, how I stayed focus and what my emotional state of mind was in all the time.

I wrote down small goals to achieve every day, as we moved towards a new way of life. I spoke into existence positive situations and scenarios, because that's what was needed for my family to hear and hold onto you on a daily basis. Your daily habits are only as effective as the discipline you use to achieve them. They go hand in hand. Without discipline, you cannot develop your daily habits.

We settled back home in Australia, and as you would expect from any good family, they rallied and gave support until we got on our feet again. To say it was hard, was an understatement.

I came to realize very quickly, that if it was meant to be, it was up to me, so for me to rebuild my life, my family, and my wealth, I had to rebuild my understanding of success.

It is now eleven years later, and I have dedicated those years to my personal growth and development, and have influenced my family through my ARMED process. I will be celebrating thirty-four years of marriage this year with the same incredible woman, who has not only inspired me to grow into my strengths, but encouraged me to follow my dreams and build upon my emotional success and financial stability again.

My children are grown and successful in their own right, and Ruth and I have become very proud grandparents as well. My career and life is a successful Motivational Speaker, Author, Leadership Coach, and Sales Coach.

My life is focused on having a positive influence in people's lives and helping them understand their success journey, not by what they achieve, but by how they feel about themselves along the way.

I have come to realize success for me is how I feel every day, and how I add value to the people around me. Success is not what I chase anymore. Happiness is the pre-curser to success, and because I am 'armed' I am happy, and success will follow.

My story is my story, and without my faith and the will to succeed, I would never had put both feet on the ground that Monday morning and made a promise to Ruth and myself that success does not define who I am in life, but it describes how I feel about myself in life.

***

To contact Bernie:

For more information on achieving success in your life contact me at www.berniegarrett.com

Tel: +61 417 422 058

Skype Name: berniefoundationleadership

https://www.facebook.com/berniegarrettofficial/

https://www.facebook.com/awarenesstogrow/

Jacqui Olliver

This entire above written information is an excerpt included in Jacqui's groundbreaking new book: Doing This ONE Thing Will Change Your Life Forever! (The ultimate guide to feeling good about living.)

Known as The Technique Modifier at End the Problem, Jacqui Olliver is considered by many to be a global expert in solving anxiety and sexual dysfunctions. In her breakthrough, Sex Mastery Programs for males and females she provides *relevant* sex education answers to solve and prevent common sex problems.

Parents of older teens should also consider purchasing the programs so:
1. The teen doesn't have the same problems inherited from ill-informed parents
2. There is a greater understanding of the complexity of sex
3. More enjoyment and rewards in active participation when you understand how it works
4. The couple complement each other, not hinder each other!
5. Take control of one of the most rewarding facets of life
6. Have a greater understanding of the instincts which enrich your life!

Acclaimed author of Doing This ONE Thing Will Change Your Life Forever!

Vital, Problem Free Sex Education
By Jacqui Olliver

There is so much confusion and conflicting messages being given, about sex and how to resolve sexual dysfunctional problems. Although excelling in teaching teens how to protect themselves during sex, the sex education system in schools is sadly lacking in helpful knowledge which prepares young adults in understanding this very important area in their lives.

It's like giving them a key, a car and a fuel voucher without teaching them the road code or the consequences of not understanding how to drive! NOTICE THE SIMILARITY?

Parents can only inform their teens with what they, themselves know. However, without explaining the complete start to end procedure required by the brain to control the sexual act, most of these well-meaning "talks" have little or no beneficial effect especially if the parents have their own sexual problems.

With that in mind, I'm devoting this in-depth chapter to help you gain a better understanding of how sexual problems occur and the requirements the brain needs to ensure a mutually fulfilling sexual act. This chapter provides real behind-the-scenes kind of insights which no-one else is telling you about.

Remember that we're not given a manual which teaches us how to "drive" our bodies, so when things go wrong (or don't work) we have nothing to compare it with.

Males tend to get their "adult" sex education from watching porn, females either from watching porn or reading romance novels. These are fairy tale scenarios based on fiction and bad examples!

For example, porn depicts women as liking it hard and fast, and a constant change of position. Yet in reality, these actions can prevent her from achieving orgasm and quite often will put her off wanting sex. If she wants hard and fast she will ask for it, if she doesn't ask, don't presume it as a prerequisite.

We have different sexual needs and preferences, yet our sex programs all work the same way.

In romance novels, an orgasm is portrayed as a massive explosion in the Universe whereas in reality it's made up of very nice, yet sometimes subtle sensations. Of course, these sensations can be deliciously intensified by applying the correct thought and action focusing sequence which is explained in my Sex Mastery program for women.

Although I started with a plethora of my own life issues and sexually related problems, I am now considered by many to be a global expert in solving anxiety and sexual dysfunctional problems.

As you will see in the statistics below, this lack of relevant knowledge leads to massive problems in our ability to relate with confidence to a partner.

Men are devastated when they can't perform sexually. And both sexes feel incomplete as a couple when they just can't seem to achieve sexual fulfilment.

Because we're not taught a complete start-to-end procedure for sex, there is a great deal of confusion involved throughout the sexual act!

Sexual dysfunctions or "malfunction" problems can occur the first time a person engages in sexual activity or they can randomly occur throughout the course of a person's life.

Our brain requires specific "messages" to activate the muscle programs related to sex. When the brain doesn't receive these signals - or the brain receives inconsistent signals, what I term sexual malfunction problems occur.

This may include erectile dysfunction, premature ejaculation and being unable to ejaculate for men. For women, common problems include randomly losing interest during sex, lack of libido, inner vaginal dryness and problems achieving orgasm.

The reported statistics:
- 30% of men suffer from premature ejaculation
- 40% of men over 40 randomly or consistently lose their erection hardness
- 80% of women have problems achieving orgasm during intercourse and 20% of that 80% fail to achieve an orgasm at all.

It is quite evident from the statistics that there are ongoing issues, for which people with problems are not receiving answers, even from so called long established experts and medicinal intervention.

Not only solving the initial problems, I can also show people the correct techniques to advance their ability in love making. What a woman needs for emotional and physical enhancement. What a man needs to regain his confidence and ability to function confidently and successfully as a participating partner.

I supply the answers for all the problems, and these are easy to understand and facilitate. There is no comparable information on the net to explain the foibles of sex and how to re-program and re-structure your brain. To regain your ability to perform normal sex… for a normal time frame… with normally expected and enjoyable results!

It's small wonder why so many people are lacking fulfilment in their relationships.

These problems often result in a low libido for either partner which is often caused by the frustrations associated with not being able to fulfil or be fulfilled during sex.

So many men and women want to be able to satisfy their partner by being able to enjoy sex and last longer in bed. They read articles and search forums, try different positions and research foods and exercises. They take drugs or medications which have unwanted side-effects (sometimes the drugs work but they feel artificial by removing the spontaneity of sex.) Others go to sex therapy or counselling, hoping for *answers.*

They feel frustrated when nothing seems to work – and they can't figure out what they're doing wrong. Often feeling tense, anxious and nervous during sex, they are desperate to have a normal sex life but it seems entirely out of reach.

For example, Nick used to ejaculate within seconds of penetration. He and his partner had tried everything – from a Urologist to a tantric master, the stop technique, the squeeze technique. Then he underwent therapy with a sex therapist as well as treatment from another world-renowned sex therapist. Every treatment he received was really expensive and did not resolve the issue.

Then he and his partner found my website. From their first communication with me, I was confident that I could solve Nick's problem – and I did. They don't have much time for sex but three weeks after his initial session he reported a beautiful encounter which lasted around 40 minutes. This was at a really intense pace. He was so happy as was his girlfriend (he reports that he's still making lots of progress.)

David found it increasingly difficult to get an erection. Combined with premature ejaculation it was so frustrating! He had tried Cialis but it stopped working and he was on medications for other health issues. He found my website while searching for answers online. What I said on my site made a great deal of sense so he booked a session.

Now, David and his girlfriend live in different States so they don't see each other often. The second week they got together after my session, he reported that things were dramatically improved. He was able to easily attain erections.

The PE issue was basically non-existent. He stayed in control and could last as long as he wanted to and reported being able to re-establish his sexual confidence.

Jean and her husband have been married for 46 years. Although Jean loved having sex because of the emotional connection and feelings of intimacy and pleasure it brought her husband, she had given up on being able to achieve an orgasm.

At the age of 76, most experts would tell her it's impossible that she would ever overcome this dilemma. However, her husband was hopeful after reading my website and they booked a session. Six weeks later, after discussing my merits at great length, they agreed what a fine thing I was doing for society. They also reported that Jean now "hits gold" nearly every time they have intercourse!

While Nick, David, and Jean's sex results look remarkable at first glance (and are definitely accomplishments to be proud of) these results aren't rocket science.

The techniques they utilized can be applied by any man or woman who wants to satisfy their partner in bed and achieve a normal, happy and spontaneous sex life.

I've coached over a thousand men and women of all ages and lifestyles, in varying states of health and fitness. And I've received reports of amazing results including:

⇒ Men with erection softness to rock hard erections to ejaculation on command

⇒ Going from ejaculating within seconds to hard and in control for over 30 mins' duration

> ⇒ Unable to orgasm, to orgasming on demand during intercourse!

It's important to be able to enjoy sex and last longer in bed so you can satisfy yourself as well as your partner. I'm going to show you the common mistakes people make when trying to restore their sex life.

As well learning a new formula for restoring your sex life, so it won't feel like it's hard work. Soon, you too can achieve a normal, happy, spontaneous sex life – and I'll show you how!

It's common for men and women who suffer from sex problems to be confused by all the options available. When trying to end the problem, it can be challenging to navigate between fact and fiction.

For example, the diet and exercise myth. What about drugs and medications? Are they safe? Do they solve the problem or are they a temporary fix? Does sex therapy actually *solve* sexual dysfunctional problems?

Many people are excited about the possibility of being able to relax and enjoy sex. To be able to comfortably enjoy the experience of sexual intimacy, so they can satisfy their partner in bed.

We've already seen that it's a possibility.

I shared Nick's story - from ejaculating within seconds of penetration to lasting around 40 minutes at what he described as a really good pace, which made his girlfriend really happy.

And David's story too – from having problems getting hard, then ejaculating early, to staying hard and in control for as long as he and his girlfriend wanted him to, all within three weeks.

Jean's result was a complete surprise to her doctor. Who would have guessed at 76 years of age she could suddenly start achieving orgasm during intercourse?

All of these things are possible! But it's impossible without the right knowledge and procedure.

When Jean and these men started out trying to solve their sex problems, they were completely overwhelmed. The guys searched on Google "how to last longer in bed" and they saw SO MANY OPTIONS.

All of them seemed like a complete lifestyle change, or something artificial which took away from the spontaneity of sex. Or it was a new and expensive type of supplement or therapy.

They all would go down the path of trying to figure out how to deal with their problem. They'd try something – and it wouldn't really work so their enthusiasm would waver. They knew they had to act, but would they ever be able to figure this out so sex could be enjoyably spontaneous and fun?

Here are some of the mistakes men and women make when they start out to solve these problems. Because there are SO many ways to go wrong when you start to figure out how to solve these problems so you can relax and enjoy a fulfilling sex life.

There are too many "experts" telling you what you want to hear, instead of what actually works. Here are the 3 biggest myths that I see many men and women fall victim to – and I want to help you avoid them:

1. "I Can Take This Drug and My Problem Will Go Away" Myth

I've had reports from hundreds of men (who had visited men's clinics, urologists, and their doctors), that erectile dysfunction and premature ejaculation drugs and medications don't work. Or they initially worked, and then they appeared to stop working. Or that they were painful, or artificial, or that the side effects were horrendous and lasted for days.

And that as soon as they stopped using the medications, their problem returned in full – sometimes worse than before. On top of these issues the generic "safe" brands can cost $15 each time you have sex!

They realized that drugs and medications don't solve the problem (and would NEVER solve the problem). Then they made a breakthrough and discovered a way to last longer so they could satisfy their partner in bed. A unique method that didn't get short term results, but enabled them to have consistently great sex. More on that soon.

2. The "Sex Therapy and Counselling" Myth

Surely a sex therapist would teach you what you need to know about lasting longer, right?

Wrong. Most sex therapists and counselors just deal with the psychological factors which can affect your sex life not the mental mechanics. This includes work-related stress and anxiety, sexual performance anxiety, marital or relationship problems, depression, feelings of guilt and the effects of past sexual trauma.

As I experienced myself, while it was helpful to talk about these things, it doesn't teach you how to solve your sexual dysfunction problem. A sex therapist may teach you about the sexual response cycle and the elements of sexual stimulation. Drugs are commonly recommended by sex therapists.

Other recommendations from sex therapy included: the squeeze technique, the stop-start technique, testosterone therapy, sprays or topical creams, Kegel exercises, penis devices, herbs, yoga, pelvic muscle exercises, sensate focus exercises, non-sexual touching techniques. As well as positively communicating your wants and desires, and learning to relax.

Therapists offer counselling, medications or techniques which only treat the symptoms. Which means that you're still left wondering if your actual problem's going to get solved or not.

These do not address the "root cause" if you will excuse the pun!

3. The "Diet and Exercise Will Help Me Last Longer" Myth

What about all those sites which state: "if you avoid these foods" or "if you eat these foods" or "exercise your penis" you'll be able to enjoy sex, last longer and satisfy your partner in bed? If so many people promise this, it has to be true, right?

Wrong. The truth is that MANY men and women eat well, exercise regularly (including Kegel exercises) and are in overall good shape. They think their sex life should be going well but it isn't.

They would start sex in the right frame of mind then a little nugget of doubt sneaks in and that thought can go in and out. Then it would snowball into a cascade of random thoughts including trying not to think about losing the erection, losing control or not being able to achieve orgasm.

These men figured there wasn't anything physically wrong because they could sometimes masturbate or have sex with a partner without any problems. They knew it must be something else, but couldn't figure it out. They wanted to stop feeling tense and anxious during sex and were hopeful for an answer.

It's important to check with a doctor to ensure any underlying health issues or medical conditions are being addressed.

In my experience, you can in most instances forget the usual sex advice. This tells you, you need to exercise, take drugs or endure months of therapy to be able to enjoy sex, last longer and satisfy your partner in bed. It's not necessary!

Instead, with advanced knowledge and a few precise "tweaks" to your current procedure during foreplay and intercourse, you can take control of your body and achieve a consistently great sex life!

Your brain needs to receive and transmit relevant messages (signals) to be able to get hard, stay hard, control ejaculation and orgasm whenever you want to. You can change how your brain reacts to the messages you give it by upgrading the information that you are storing in your brain.

Which is why aligning your thoughts and actions is so important.

My unique Sex Mastery programs will help men and women who suffer from sex problems gain the skills and confidence to have a spontaneous, normal and happy sex life. These programs will also help older teens *prevent* these common sex problems from occurring. So, all can relax, enjoy sex and satisfy their partner in bed without it feeling like it's doomed to failure!

***

To Contact Jacqui:

Get The 5 Crucial Rules of Sex at https://www.endtheproblem.com/rules

Sex Mastery Programs for Men and Women: https://www.endtheproblem.com/programs

End the Problem Website: https://www.endtheproblem.com

Email Jacqui: jacqui@endtheproblem.com

LinkedIn: https://nz.linkedin.com/in/jacquiolliver

Facebook: https://www.facebook.com/EndTheProblem

Twitter: https://twitter.com/endtheproblem

Evelyn Wang

Evelyn Wang, C.Ht. provides remarkably effective solutions for those ready to experience empowering shifts in their lives with results-oriented Creating Your Future® Coaching, and other proven systems that facilitate fast, long-term change.

As a practitioner and teacher of the art and science of change, she helps others discover how to make better use of their natural "inner technology" to enhance the quality of their lives.

Evelyn specializes in Personal Breakthroughs because people find the benefits cross over to all areas of their lives, solving much more than just "the problem".

This means that not only does she address "the problem", she addresses the whole person. It's a more functional approach. And it can be life-changing.

She is Board Certified as a Hypnotherapist, Instructor of Hypnotherapy, Master Coach and NLP Trainer—with a Diploma in Clinical Hypnotherapy. Evelyn is also certified as a Fitness Nutrition Specialist and skilled in various "mind-body" healing modalities.

Private coaching is available in person at her Los Angeles office, and by phone with clients worldwide. Evelyn is fluent in English, Mandarin and Taiwanese.

Bridging The Divide Within

By Evelyn Wang

Ever wonder why people do the things they do?

More often than not, it's because they learned to.

So, how does one begin to change what no longer works for them?

By committing oneself to learning something new.

We've all learned many things in our lives. And we all have many resources that have (consciously) been long forgotten. But they're still there, stored deep in your mind. In fact, I'd like to suggest that you can be much more resourceful than you may think.

Resourcefulness is defined as "having the ability to find quick and clever ways to overcome difficulties".

I believe that people already have the resources within themselves that they need in order to achieve their desired outcomes. They just need to learn how to tap into them.

Do you remember staring at all those squiggly shapes and lines positioned above the chalkboard on your first day of school? The 26 letters of the alphabet. Remember the challenge before you to make sense of all that?

But you achieved it, didn't you? You learned to read and write. Did you forget what a great learner you are? Remember.

Learning is one of your greatest strengths. And choosing — for yourself —what and how you want to learn (or unlearn) is a big part of waking up to your true power.

I began learning to read and speak English when I was eight years old after my family moved from the island of Taiwan to the tiny island of Guam. (My native languages are Taiwanese and Mandarin.)

When I was sixteen, we immigrated to California. Moving to America was an eye-opening experience. I've always had a curious mind. I was eager to explore. And explore I did!

I grew up in a strict Asian household where, let's just say, my independent spirit and preference for learning things my own way was not well received. In other words, I was the rebel in my family. Defying limitations and "coloring outside the lines" were my specialties. And experience was my unfailing teacher.

> **"You don't learn to walk by following rules. You learn by doing, and by falling over."**
>
> —RICHARD BRANSON

We've all—to varying degrees—had our perceptions managed since the day we were born, by a wide range of external influences. But you can begin to wake up to your own innate power to change the quality of your perceptions and truly improve the quality of your life.

There is simply no better improvement you can make than to gain greater control over your internal mental and emotional processes. It's directly related to your ability to be resourceful.

But how does one go about doing that?

In Chinese medicine, it's said that the cause of all disease is a conflict between "two wills". This creates division, which in turn creates dis-ease.

This division has been expressed in many ways:

- head and heart
- body and mind
- left brain and right brain
- flesh and spirit
- reason and imagination

- conscious mind and unconscious mind

As a mind coach, I've helped many break free from their limiting, so-called "realities" in life and learn exactly how to create more compelling futures for themselves. And my work has largely involved helping others integrate this division within themselves.

"Patients are patients because they are out of rapport with their own unconscious."

—MILTON ERICKSON, MD

You have a conscious mind, and you have a unconscious mind. By working holistically with both, you encourage whole brain thinking, which maximizes your strengths, flexibility and resourcefulness.

Ever notice how the "smartest" people in your life sometimes do "not-so-smart" things? That's because intelligence and behavior are two different matters entirely!

There's a big difference between one's intellect (their conscious mind) and their behavior (their unconscious, or habitual mind). It's the difference between "talking the talk" (desired behavior) and "walking the walk" (actual behavior). It's the difference that makes the difference.

"Your conscious mind is that part of you that picks up the pieces of what your unconscious is doing."

—CAROLINE MYSS

There's a large amount of truth in the saying "if you always do what you've always done, you'll always get what you've always gotten".

Or, as Albert Einstein once said, "You can't solve a problem from the same mindset that created it. You must learn to see the world anew." And learning that is a process.

Sometimes a person doesn't always know exactly what to do to make the change and improvement they need in their lives. Deep down, they know they can do it, but they stumble around a bit, trying this and that.

Though books, workshops and other forms of self-help can certainly be valuable tools toward the process of change, they often serve as a temporary band aid over the deeper unconscious issues in one's life. In other words, if you don't find a way to address the deeper issues in your life, you may unconsciously keep repeating the same mistakes over and over again (otherwise known as "suffering").

The good news: You have a "treasure chest" hidden deep within your mind that can allow you to create some very effective changes in your life within a relatively short period of time. It's called your unconscious (or subconscious) mind. And it's considered to be the source of your motivation, habits, behaviors, attitudes, emotions, and self-talk.

Working one-on-one with a competent person who's been trained to work effectively with the unconscious mind can exponentially speed up a person's learning process.

Neuro-Linguistic Programming (NLP), hypnotherapy and Time Line Therapy™ are a few examples of modalities that work with the unconscious mind.

NLP, for instance, works with clients as unique individuals—instead of trying to fit them into theories. Consider this: If I'm too busy wondering which "box" you fit in, have I ever really understood how you uniquely create your problem for yourself?

If you work with someone highly trained in NLP, you won't spend a lot of time wallowing in the content of "the problem". The focus will be on how you uniquely process that content. And they will quickly help you to gain profound insight, resolve old patterns; and let go of the negativity, limiting beliefs, and inner conflicts that are blocking happiness, prosperity and success from your life.

> **"Each person is a unique individual. Therapy should be formulated to meet the uniqueness of the individual's needs, rather than tailoring the person to fit the hypothetical theory of human behavior."**
>
> —MILTON ERICKSON, MD

Those who lack an understanding of the unique, deeper structures within the unconscious mind of the person they're helping can certainly give them a lot of conscious concepts that appeal to that person's intellect, or conscious mind (about 10% of the mind, the "tip of the iceberg").

Unfortunately, however, this can sometimes sound to the person like a bunch of platitudes, without any precise methods to increase their motivation and to get their desired results. (A lot of "what", and not a lot of "how".)

The fact is: Most significant behavioral change occurs with the involvement and cooperation of the habitual, or unconscious mind (the other 90% of "the iceberg").

Someone skilled in NLP will not impose their "model of the world" onto their clients, or limit their clients (and therefore their results with them) by putting them "in a box" (or theory). They will work within their client's "model of the world" (subjective experience) and help them to discover the solutions that are already there.

Human beings don't thrive well in boxes. They do, however, when they learn how to break free of them.

Therapeutic hypnosis also provides an ideal environment for learning new things.

> **"Hypnosis is a heightened sense of suggestibility for accessing the subconscious mind which is responsible for up to 90 to 95 percent of our thoughts and actions."**
>
> —THE WASHINGTON TIMES

My first experience with hypnosis was through attending a stage show. The show was at a hotel near where the Oakland Raiders football team was practicing. And some of the players were in the audience. I watched these big football players go up on stage and do the most hilarious things—such as twirling around like ballerinas!

Needless to say, I was entertained, but I was also intrigued. Little did I know, I would later go on to become a hypnotherapist.

Hypnotherapy is the use of hypnosis as a therapeutic technique. It's been approved by the American Medical Association since 1958. And it's long been known as an effective, evidence-based solution for stress, habit control and self-improvement.

Therapeutic hypnosis isn't the same as "stage" hypnosis. Stage hypnosis is performed solely for the purpose of entertaining an audience. Therapeutic hypnosis is performed in a clinical setting—with your best interests in mind—by a hypnotherapist, solely for the purpose of helping you meet your desired outcome.

"Even though stage hypnotists and TV shows have damaged the public image of hypnosis, a growing body of scientific research supports its benefits in treating a wide range of conditions, including pain, depression, anxiety and phobias."

—AMERICAN PSYCHOLOGICAL ASSOCIATION

How'd you know to be you when you got up this morning? Your unconscious mind is a lot like a database that runs patterns of behavior—largely independent of your conscious mind—based on your programming from your past. In other words, you're "on auto-pilot" the majority of your day.

Hypnotherapy accesses and unlocks this powerful part of the mind in order to help you quickly and easily change (or "re-write") your old programming and patterns of behavior.

"The purpose of hypnosis as a therapeutic technique is to help you understand and gain more control over your behavior, emotions or physical well-being."

—THE MAYO CLINIC

When you want to make a change or improvement in your life, the logic of your conscious mind alone—without the cooperation of the motivation from your unconscious mind—is often ineffective. (In other words, you "say it", but you don't "do it".)

Hypnotherapy can help you to effectively change habits of an entire lifetime and to create a healthier reality for yourself.

"Hypnosis is the epitome of mind-body medicine. It can enable the mind to tell the body how to react, and modify the messages that the body sends to the mind."

—THE NEW YORK TIMES

A comparative study published in *Psychotherapy Magazine*, v7n1 and in *Psychotherapy: Theory, Research, and Practice* found hypnotherapy to be one of the most effective of all the major therapeutic approaches:

Psychoanalysis: 38% recovery after 600 sessions

Cognitive Behavioral Therapy: 72% recovery after 22 sessions

Hypnotherapy: 93% recovery after 6 sessions

Hypnotherapy is an impressive choice in terms of (1) the cost, (2) the short duration of therapy, and (3) the results.

"I think it should be much more widely used. It's safe, it's inexpensive and it can produce dramatic results."

—DR. ANDREW WEIL

Because of the often ridiculous way it's often been portrayed in the media, some mistakenly think it isn't safe. However, the fact is:

Therapeutic hypnosis has helped millions of people to create healthy change in their lives for the past 60 years.

It's completely safe, relaxing, enjoyable and surprisingly effective.

"Hypnosis is not mind control. It's a naturally occurring state of concentration; It's actually a means of enhancing your control over both your mind and your body—over perceptions such as pain, anxiety, habits, stress."

—DR. DAVID SPIEGEL, Stanford University School of Medicine

The state of hypnosis is a very natural, real, normal state of mind. In essence, it's a receptive learning state. And it's not so different from the state you're in when you're watching a good movie, daydreaming, enjoying an interesting book, being overwhelmed by the beauty of nature, or listening to song that moves you.

"Contrary to how hypnosis is sometimes portrayed, you don't lose control over your behavior while under hypnosis. You generally remain aware of and remember what happens under hypnosis."

—THE MAYO CLINIC

It's basically paying attention, while feeling increasing levels of relaxation. During hypnotherapy, you'll remain completely aware of everything that's going on, as you're guided through some beneficial imaginative processes; so:

- Don't expect to feel "hypnotized".
- Do expect to feel relaxed.
- You won't say or do anything you don't want to.
- You're in total control.

Your natural ability to go into relaxed states of focused awareness is utilized and enhanced through hypnotherapy for the purpose of helping you access, unlock and reprogram the deeper, motivating areas of your mind. And the results are: welcome changes in your behavior.

"Though often denigrated as fakery or wishful thinking, hypnosis has been shown to be a real phenomenon with a variety of therapeutic uses…"

—SCIENTIFIC AMERICAN

Anyone can experience therapeutic hypnosis if they're willing to, and can follow simple instructions. Those who claim they "can't be hypnotized" usually (1) have yet to be informed about what therapeutic hypnosis actually is, and/or (2) are just unwilling to "be hypnotized".

It's a "do with" process, not a "do to" process.

"I believe hypnosis has profound powers to help you stop sabotaging yourself."

—DR. OZ

Right now, you possess three very powerful gifts:

CHOICE, FOCUS, and IMAGINATION.

How do you choose to perceive external events? Do you habitually hand the "remote control" to your emotional life over to others?

Are you aware that you are choosing your reactions and the meanings you give to external events?

"The greatest weapon against stress is your ability to choose one thought over another."

—WILLIAM JAMES

If you want personal power in your life, it's essential that you realize you are, always. Recovering the role of choice in your life is one of the greatest things you can do for yourself.

Often we have to deal with situations which are not within our control. How we choose to perceive them, however, is where we do have control.

Developing the habit of living consciously, choice by choice, is much more empowering than habitually blaming things outside yourself as the reasons for your challenges in life. (Remember: "No choice" is a choice.)

An elderly woman looked in the mirror one morning. She'd been experiencing a lot of hair loss over several years and today she discovered that she only had three remaining hairs on her head. Being a "glass half full" kind of person, she said, "I think I'll braid my hair today." So she braided her three remaining hairs, and set out to have a great day.

Some days later, looking in the mirror as she prepared for her day, she saw she only had two hairs remaining now. "Hmm, I'm going to have a part in the center today." She parted her two hairs, and made the decision to enjoy her day.

A week or so later, she saw that she had just one hair left on her head. "One hair huh....," she chuckled, "I know, a pony-tail will be perfect." And again she busied herself with enjoying her day.

The next morning, she looked in the mirror. She was completely bald. "Finally bald," she said to herself, "How wonderful! I won't have to waste time doing my hair anymore!"

"Always remember, your focus determines your reality."

—GEORGE LUCAS

Do you control your emotional state, or does your emotional state control you? It's said that "energy flows where attention goes". Where is your attention, or focus—internally? Because that focus determines your results.

To gain inner influence, you must first be aware of where your focus is.

It's estimated that a person has between 60,000 - 90,000 thoughts a day. How many of those are recycled thoughts? How many are helpful thoughts? How many are focused on what you want? And how many are focused on what you don't want?

As we think, we form images in our mind. Understand that your thoughts contain sight, sound, feelings—even smell and taste. This is also known as imagination.

One of the key components of true success in life is the ability to consciously direct your imagination rather than being unconsciously directed by it.

> **"Imagination is more important than knowledge."**
>
> —ALBERT EINSTEIN

For example, if a teenager was experiencing anxiety about an upcoming test, she could be: seeing her parents disapproving looks; hearing their angry voices; feeling ashamed; and telling herself that she's a failure. That's where her focus and imagination would be in that moment (and she may only be conscious of the anxiety).

But where would she like it to be? Because she has the innate potential to direct her focus. It's a habit that can be developed.

As a replacement, she could be seeing herself getting her test back with an "A" on it, hearing her parents compliment her; feeling satisfaction; and telling herself that she's a success.

Now—of course—she's still going to have to take the necessary actions to do what she has to do to make that happen as well (study, etc). Taking action externally is as important as learning the internal process of focusing on what you want.

The point is that many people are constantly forming images in their minds that they are largely unconscious of. And they are building a big part of their "reality" with these images.

If you don't ever specify what you want (because you're too busy staying in touch with what you don't want) common sense would tell you that it's less achievable, wouldn't it?

Becoming conscious of where your internal focus and imagination are will always be primary to creating what you want in your life. And it's a key to controlling your emotional state. Excellent results require excellent states.

What if you began to consider that many of the unhelpful emotions you feel are actually alerts to you that, internally, you're focusing on what you don't want. The unconscious use of your imagination. And what if that alert was a helpful reminder for you to begin consciously directing your focus toward what you want?

You can learn how. Life is learning.

***

To contact Evelyn:

Email: evelyn@evelyntwang.com

Phone: (818) 532-1511

Websites: www.evelyntwang.com

https://centerforadvancedlifeskills.com

Facebook: https://www.facebook.com/evelyntwang

Twitter: https://twitter.com/evelyntwang

Scott Sadler

Scott Sadler is an executive coach for CEOs and top executives who want to manage the pressure to perform and have high functioning teams. As a keynote speaker and corporate trainer, he cares deeply about enhancing the most vital and expensive aspect in business, human capital.

Scott believes all problems ultimately have a communication solution. This is why he is known as *The Millennial Mentor*. This young generation is both valuable and disruptive to the workplace, and their leaders are failing to integrate them. Scott demonstrates how to relate to each generation, so everyone can feel stable, profitable, and purposeful.

In 2014, Scott's book was published, *"A Guide for Developing Successful Millennial Leaders."* He's currently the Director of Workplace Programs for the Executive Coaching University, serving 38 countries. He was also recognized in 2011 as "New Business of the Year" by the Salem Area Chamber of Commerce.

Here's a video of Scott in action. https://youtu.be/Z-xrCqgW-KI

5 Mindful Questions That Lead to Success

By Scott Sadler

1. Has "busy" become your default mode?

When someone asks how you are doing, do you frequently reply, "Busy!" This has become an acceptable response in our society, almost a badge of honor. You might think busy implies that you're successful, in-demand, or a multi-tasking superstar. But what if it caused others to question your ability to set boundaries, prioritize your time, and practice self-care? Heck, some might even assume that you are looking for sympathy or too busy to hear about an opportunity that could include you!

Let's step back and examine how "busy" has become glamourized. Since humans first showed up on Earth, we have been evolving at a steady pace. Twelve thousand years ago, we lived as hunters and gatherers. This was the first and most successful human adaptation. The financial-agricultural revolution created settlements to support our growing population. When we moved into the industrial revolution and the manufacturing processes began, incredible advancements were made. With each leap forward as a species, our efficiencies increased by at least fifty percent. Progress continued into the scientific-technical revolution, the information-telecommunications revolution, and today, we are immersed in the internet revolution. Never in history have we been pummeled with so much information and so many tasks.

If busy has become your default mode, notice when you flippantly exclaim that you're busy. How else can you respond? Be more precise about what you're doing, instead of using generic terms. Try phrases like, "I'm engaged in some incredible projects at work," or "The kids and I have been having fun shopping for the holidays." People appreciate specificity and real life examples.

Studies suggest that nearly 80% of disease in the United States has its origin in stress. This is why it's crucial to develop boundaries and learn how to communicate them. Try saying "no" as part of your self-care ritual. Ask your body, mind, and soul what it needs each day. Trust what you hear and act on it.

True Story: For the last 30 years as an entrepreneur, I've prided myself on being of assistance when my clients and colleagues are in need. In 2007, I felt burned out and unhappy because I was focused on pleasing everyone but me. For years, I had dreamed of doing a 2-week nature retreat where I'd get to live in the wilderness and learn primitive survival skills. I kept delaying registration because I was much too busy. I also thought that my trip would be viewed as indulgent and low on the scales of importance. One day, I impulsively signed up and then told my staff, wife, and business partners that I was leaving. No one was happy with me, but if I chose not to go, I knew the outcomes could be grave.

Within hours of breathing nature's fresh air, I realized that I didn't have access to my day-to-day life for the first time in years. My focus was on the present moment. Each day, I would go to my "sit spot" and just sit. I was alone with nothing but the sounds of the forest. I could feel myself healing, I kid you not. I had spent too much time in my man-made environment with my man-made issues. Nature reprogramed my system and restored my fortitude like nothing else.

If you long for a break, do not ignore it. Take action to support your inner peace and happiness. Your outer world will thank you, and you'll join the ranks of those with excellent self-awareness who know what they need to thrive.

2. Do you know what it means to "just be?"

Interest in meditation has hit an all-time high, yet most people find it nearly impossible to turn off their mind chatter and enter this elusive state of stillness. If you think you're alone in the struggle, you are actually in the vast majority. It's important to recognize that American culture rewards those who are active. We praise and marvel at people's hard-earned efforts, mental breakthroughs, epiphanies, and physical achievements. So what's the point of just being?

Being is an optimal state of mind and we've been taught to approach it backwards. We were told that if we "have" more things like time, money, or fame, then we can finally "do" what we've always wanted to do, such as take vacations, start a business, or buy a new house. This leads us to "be" who we've always dreamed we could be: joyful, satisfied, loved, and healthy.

In order to "be" you must get quiet for a period of time each day and try to wipe the slate clean. Allow a blank wall to exist in your mind that has no words and no agenda. Think of it as breathing space for your talents, curiosity, and higher self to emerge. Yoga, prayer, and deep breathing are excellent means to accomplish this.

When you practice going inside, it helps to have zero expectation of accomplishing anything. When we create these gaps in our thoughts and interrupt cerebral activity, its benefits can be immediate and immense.

True Story: As a 15 year daily meditator, I can attest to the power of quiet time in my personal and business life. As a young person, I was high strung, impatient, and had a quick temper. Meditation has shown me how to relax, focus on my breath, and just be. Even ten minutes per day can revolutionize how I view the world and myself. The first few meditation classes were absolutely excruciating. My neck and back were killing me, and I wanted to scream and bolt from the room.

My experiences varied until I reached the point where calmness was visibly creeping into my daily routine. My staff saw the difference. My family took notice. I was less involved in things that at one time seemed a big deal. Eventually, I started sharing my "quiet time practices" with my coaching clients and corporate training participants. The results were palpable: conflict resolved more quickly, communication was intentional and clear, and day-to-day stressors could be easily diminished.

As for me, my entire life has positively pivoted based on this one decision to go within every single day. It sets the tone for dealing with the outside world. On the rare occasion that I don't meditate, the day feels more frantic. It's like forgetting to brush my teeth in the morning. I don't want to get too close to anyone! Each day, I set the timer and make my "quiet time" non-negotiable. There are some terrific resources available for learning meditation. Two of my favorite meditation apps are Insight Timer and Headspace.

3. How do you thank your body for its ability to move?

None of us need to be convinced that exercise is a good thing for us. It can seem almost cliché to suggest fitness as a form of self-care, but it bears repeating. "Exercise is the single best thing you can do for your brain in terms of mood, memory, and listening," said Harvard Medical School psychiatrist, John Ratey. Even ten minutes changes your brain. With the release of serotonin, dopamine, and norepinephrine, you can get chilled out, pumped up, and almost feel buzzed, naturally. Some studies say that exercise reverses the detrimental effects of stress. According to a 2010 study from the University of California—San Francisco, researchers found that exercise helps us to ruminate less on our worries. It alternates blood flow to areas of the brain that replay stressful thoughts, again and again. Knowing this, it's hard to understand why we don't jump at the chance to hit the gym.

If you were in a room with top executives and CEOs, you would find that the majority of them exercise regularly, usually first thing in the morning. A common leadership trait is to take exquisite care of yourself. They know that in order to be their best, they have to get their blood flowing and sweat dripping. Physical movement is energizing and it makes you feel good about yourself.

Even a brisk walk is better than nothing. Studies show that workers who take time to exercise on a regular basis are more productive and have more vitality than their sedentary counterparts. Some experts believe that midday is the ideal time for a workout because of the body's circadian rhythms. Regardless of when you choose, give yourself this gift!

If you've ever been around physically disabled folks, perhaps you've viewed your body with more gratitude and realized that you're capable of increasing your fitness. Sometimes, we forget how good we have it compared to others. Next time you're debating whether you want to break a sweat, decide to thank your body with exercise and let it know that you appreciate all it does for you!

True story: I was never much of gym guy, except to play pickup basketball. This was my exercise and outlet for relieving stress. When I sold my business and relocated, my established fitness routine came to a halt. For years, I tried a variety of activities, but nothing would stick. Fitness had become a chore rather than a treat. Eventually, I started running, but with a purpose this time. I had discovered trail running and found a training partner. We did our first Ultra Marathon, a 50k (31.2 miles) in the coastal hills near my home in Oregon. While I felt that it was an amazing feat for me physically, the intensity of the training had benefitted me in other ways too. My creativity was off the charts, my sleep was deeply restful, and I had a sense of confidence and peace that I had never known before.

While I have never considered myself to be an anxious person, I realized through running that I *did* have fears that were lurking below the surface. Exhausting myself physically would either melt them away or give me clarity to know what to do about them. When my partner had to break our training regime, it took about six weeks to notice that my memory, creativity, and motivation had taken a severe nosedive. Everything *is interconnected.* Quiet time is related to your physical activity, which is related to your sleep, and that is related to your mental sharpness, balance, and overall energy level. Begin moving your body today. It is never too late and you will never regret it.

4. Do you know how to lead different kinds of people?

Harvard Fellow, Caitlin C. Rosenthal, studied accounting books from the mid-1800s as part of her research on the history of business practices. What she learned was alarming. Can you believe there are management practices that are widely used today that were created by slave owners? *("From Slavery to Scientific Management: Capitalism and Control in America, 1754-1911,"* and, *"Slavery's Capitalism.")* The way we manage has evolved on some levels, but the underlying motivators haven't changed much. Leaders always want to get more from their people, while minimizing the company's expense. Strategic coaching is the best way to do this!

Coaching isn't about cheering on your team. It's a specific skillset that honors what each person needs to feel motivated and productive. Strong coaching is a streamlined and sustainable practice because at its core, you are treating people as people, not as a means to an end. Millennials, in particular, respond very well to being coached, as opposed to carrot and stick incentives.

Let's explore why coaching works.

(1.) It is a co-creative relationship. There is no coaching if the "coachee" is not interested in participating. I used to donate my coaching services from time to time and without financial commitment, my free clients missed appointments and did not follow through as well as those who were invested in the process.

(2.) Agreement and accountability are essential. Since coaching is co-creative, there must be an agreed upon goal and desired outcome.

This allows difficult conversations or disciplinary action to organically arise because it's addressing the goal at hand.

(3.) Validation opens lines of trust. Brain expert, Robin Rose, says "Validate people at every given opportunity." This allows them to feel better about themselves, about you, and about their environment. Then, if they make a mistake or require a tough conversation, they will already know they are valued, which will help them be open to feedback.

(4.) Ask permission-based questions. "Would you mind if I offered a few suggestions?" or "I hear what you are saying. May I let you know my perspective?" These questions open curiosity and permit the ensuing conversation to be held in a non-threating environment.

True Story: I was once hired by the CEO of a financial institution. He asked me to work with a V.P. who was building walls of alienation. Collaboration had been stymied on his team and his people were afraid to express their opinions, or question how things were done. In my first few sessions with "Jack" it was clear that he wanted to be liked. He could not understand why he was perceived as being toxic. He was good in his role, but he lacked the ability to meaningfully connect with others. Sometimes, he was even merciless. His first assignment was to begin a daily walkabout. Leave his office, grab a cup of coffee, and visit with his department. No agenda, just small talk, validation, permission-based questions, and an intention to listen without the need to fix or respond. This was uncomfortable for Jack, but he was blown away by the changes it evoked. Soon Jack started to understand the people side of business. He built trust with his staff and it quickly boosted his team's efficiency and willingness to collaborate.

This level of self-awareness happened for Jack because the CEO had hired a coach to help him see it. The CEO had every right to discipline him and even fire him for his actions. Instead, he found a coach for Jack that would benefit him and the entire organization, for years to come.

5. Are you true to yourself in every decision you make?

I've heard it said that humans are emotional beings, but experience tells me otherwise. I believe humans are *value based* beings. When we ignore our values for a perceived reward, the end result is usually emotional. Values are the inherent ways in which we live our lives: humility, determination, respect, integrity, or humor. This topic alone provokes potent changes for people because it gives them a bottom line from which to base all their decisions. If a choice is not aligned with your values, there's no debate needed. It's not in your best interest to say yes and if you do, there will likely be consequences. As part of my coaching and training process, I do a values assessment to learn everyone's unique ways. We often share similar values with each other, but they might rank differently in importance. Learning this information about your boss, partner, coworker, friend, or family member can significantly enhance your interactions with them. When you know what's important to others and vice versa, you can honor each other's requests with kindness and clarity.

If you haven't discovered your own core values, start there. Choose four or five to begin, so you can easily see what's important to you. Don't confuse values and goals. A value is an internal belief, while a goal is something specific that you want to accomplish, like running a marathon or losing 20 lbs. The advantage to naming your values first is that you avoid setting a goal that would negatively conflict with your values. Another thing to be mindful of when choosing values is to pick ones that you sincerely care about, rather than ones that are socially acceptable or that you feel you "should" choose. This is a time to be 100%, unapologetically yourself. It's your life, after all.

Living from your values comes with a warning. There's a purging process that usually takes place where the people, places, and things that don't fit your values, no longer fit into your life. Let them go! Now that you understand how to create harmony for yourself, you'll be able to spot the right opportunities and immediately say yes!

True Story: I am living my values today, but that wasn't always the case. I went through years of making bad decisions and surrounding myself with people who did not have the ability to help me grow or improve. While I had lowered my bar, I still had this inner voice nudging me to make a better choice. It was like an angel on my shoulder saying, "Fine! Go ahead because this isn't going to last forever!" In my 20s and into my 30s, I made some major changes and it all began when I examined my values. From there, I was able to clean up my circle of influence and find meaning in my future.

These five "Mindful Questions That Lead to Success" are designed to help you stop unconscious patterns, slow down your speed, encourage exercise and coaching, and know what decisions will ultimately serve you best.

1. Has "busy" become your default mode?

2. Do you know what it means to "just be?"

3. How do you thank your body for its ability to move?

4. Do you know how to lead different kinds of people?

5. Are you are true to yourself in every decision you make?

These questions will refine your path to success and bring calm into every aspect of your existence. You may find that it's easy to get swept up in complaining, gossiping, and criticizing of yourself and others. Write these questions down and post on your wall. They will snap you out of habitual negative thinking and bring you back to the person you want to be, and the things that matters most.

***

To contact Scott:

https://www.sadlerrosetraining.com/

http://creative-conflict-solutions.com/

https://www.linkedin.com/in/scottsadlercoach/

https://www.facebook.com/scott.sadler1

https://twitter.com/1trustedadviser

Phone: 971-600-3856

Chad Steven

After graduating from college with a degree in finance, Chad was left wanting more information on topics outside of his area of study.

As part of the millennial generation, he has made it one of his goals to be a leader amongst his peers. He is an avid practitioner of peak performance and has developed an understanding of physiology and the biochemistry of the human body.

With his many journeys around the world, he has become fascinated with human behavior which has transferred over into his career and other areas of his life.

"Chad has the knowledge of someone far beyond his years. One of his gifts is his constant search for like-minded people and new information." Amazing things happen when like-minded people work together to solve a common goal. A crucial component for achieving any goal is to take deliberate action towards the outcome as often as possible.

Accomplishment Through Action

By Chad Steven

How many of us have tried to do something, and after a few days or a week of high motivation, that determination dwindles and we are back at square one? That is because will power and motivation never last when you are doing something without a clear idea of what the ideal outcome is.

I personally wanted to run a marathon. Long distance running is not something that I enjoyed very much but I wanted to run a marathon to prove to myself that I could. So, I started to run. I would run two miles, then three, then after a week I might do five miles. When I took a day off or let something get in the way of running, I would slowly stop all together. Many similar scenarios like this happened throughout my life, as I'm sure many people can relate to. Once I started to learn about how vital a detailed plan is to achieving goals, I went back to the drawing board. This time I wanted to run a marathon and what did I do? I signed up for a marathon that was six weeks out from the day I registered, without having done any training. This created pull for me; I physically spent the $150.00 to register and now the goal was something tangible. I went 2 steps further and purchased some long distance running shoes for another $100.00. Also, I made a calendar with the exact distances I would run each day with appropriate rest in between them. Long story short, I completed that marathon and although the actual race was still challenging, each day that I completed longer distances, the less daunting this once farfetched goal became. In the week before the marathon, I had easily run 16 miles and there was no longer a fraction of a doubt in my mind that I could run a marathon.

Guess what? After running the marathon, I felt great, but doves didn't fly out when I finished and there wasn't an extravagant party in which everyone was praising me for my greatness. In fact, I drove myself to the marathon, completed it, and drove back home as if nothing had happened. The reason I say that is because that is what happens for most of the goals we complete. It is important to know that the world won't stop spinning when you achieve your goals (usually). If financial wealth is your goal, you'll start to take practical steps to get there and you will reach a point you once thought was successful, but you are already looking further up the latter. That is a beautiful thing because it allows for continued evolution. Knowing that each goal is only part of a bigger picture, it is important to focus on developing all areas of our lives with greater fulfillment.

So how does this relate to taking action and surrounding ourselves with influential people? Since action and execution are your mental muscles, once you start to use them, they will become stronger. So just go and do. If you want to meet someone, send them an email and tell them what little information you do know. Be honest. Do this with ten different people tonight, then meet with those people who respond and let them humble you with how little you truly know about a given field. Then take that inspiration and continue to learn. If you want to get better at public speaking, take a video of yourself with a smartphone and start explaining something that you are passionate about. Rewatch the video, critique it and practice some more. Sign up for the next Toastmasters group or send an email to local college clubs and tell them you have a great presentation you want to give for ten minutes. Speak in front of a group of eager twenty-somethings. You'll stumble on your words and say "um" two-thousand times. It's going to feel terrible in the moment but then you'll leave, work on what you did wrong and within a week of giving a presentation every day you will be monumentally better than 95% of people. Most importantly, YOU will see improvement.

When I decided to be a part of this book series, I was debating between writing topics. I went back into my mental archive and started to search for some key pieces of advice or key events that had a significant, positive impact on my life. I was writing down things like, "Surround yourself with the people you aspire to be" and "You can do anything you set your mind to". When I had a page or so of quotes and topics that I thought were the most impactful in my life, I started to realize that none of those were the core reason for real change in my life. So now what? Let's look at the core of all the words of wisdom that can be found on the internet: "Surround yourself with influential people" Well, how do you go about doing that? How do you get in contact with people when you are a novice at something but want to provide value for them? How do you figure out how to make it worth their time? How do we surround ourselves with these people and how do we start to make incremental improvements in our lives? You create pull. Creating pull is about finding and doing things that are pulling you towards your goal rather than you having to push against an obstacle to get to where you want to be. It all revolves around action. many successful people who I have been privileged enough to talk to are experts when it comes to action and execution. Action and execution are mental muscles that will get stronger over time. Taking action towards business, health, and your social life is difficult at the start, hectic in the middle, but it is absolutely beautiful at the end.

Let's get really meta with this topic and talk about this book right now. I always wanted to write a book, but it seemed utterly unattainable. Who would read it? What would I write about? Am I even good at writing? I am comfortable saying that I am not a good writer (yet). I have no practice with writing aside from a few projects throughout my schooling. But, I committed to writing a chapter in this book and I got it done. I am technically a published author now, and whether this book sells ten million or zero copies, I have put my name on a book and learned the process of what goes into getting a book published. Writing a book on my own is no longer a daunting goal. It will still be hard when I decide to write a whole book, but as

I did for this chapter, I will set a goal, make a commitment, and create specific steps to completion. Don't over-think it, deliberately practice your craft and always strive for improvement. There truly is no right time for anything.

Here comes my rah-rah motivation but I am going to take it one step further and offer practical solutions and steps you can use. The studies on automaticity have been out for a while now. Automaticity is the formation of a habit. The studies show that average habit plateaus are reached after 66 days. The length has been up for debate; some say it's thirty days, some say its six weeks. We are going to stick with 66 days because if it is less than that, then a few extra days will only solidify that habit. Everyone can decide what works for their personality and lifestyle but there are a few key habits that need to be included daily and weekly into all our lives. Those are exercise, education, and food. There are more and there are less but I am casting a broad net here.

Exercise

Exercise has so many benefits and I would recommend that everyone start to learn about them. To give a summary: exercise lowers your stress hormone, increases the 'feel good' hormone dopamine, and can positively affect physical appearance which adds a boost of confidence. The benefit that I find to be the most beneficial is the effect that exercise has on brain health and cognition. Exercise increases oxygen to the brain, and creates something called brain-derived neurotrophic factor (BDNF). BDNF is a key protein for healthy brain function. Creating a habit of exercising opens many opportunities as well. Aside from using a gym, you can go for a hike, swim, rock climbing, or practice yoga. I'm sure you see the many benefits of exercise, so start by making a detailed plan or ideal outcome for exercise and get going. Go out and buy workout shoes and sign-up for a membership so that you are committed. If you want to give yourself more pull, get a workout partner so that you have someone to hold you accountable in reaching your goals.

Education

Education is a never-ending process. Some of the best information can be found outside of a formal setting or school. Great leaders and successful people are always learning. Invest in knowledge even if it isn't free. It is easy to get a book recommendation from a trusted source and not buy it because it costs money. There is great information available both for free and for a fee. You will go through tons of books and information sources and some are going to completely waste your time. Set those aside and pick up new sources. When you need to learn marketing for your business, doing a web search for "how to do marketing" and reading one article is not research. Read that article and ten others, email the authors and ask where they learned this information, then go and read other works by those people. Challenging someone who says, "you know, THEY say you should do X, Y, and Z if you start a business" is key. Who are 'they'? Is that your friend, coworker, mother, father, boss, or someone you overheard at a restaurant? Take multiple sources of information and look for common themes, and then start to develop your own thoughts on the topic. With some exception, if you are reading this book, chances are you are undoubtedly capable of learning and mastering a skill. Find the topic that you are geniunely interested in. This unforced learning is going to allow you to become an authority much quicker than trying to learn something forcefully. It's not all fun and games but once you reach a state of automaticity with your habit for learning, the process of looking for something new to learn will become more enjoyable.

Food.

What you put in your body has a huge impact on your life. Many people don't realize that a "food coma" should not be a goal when you eat. When you go into a "food coma" your body is essentially telling you "you need to lay down because I can't process all of this right now". The cheat day once a week or a few times per month is fine. But proper nutrition should be able to give you energy to last for 12-16 hours a day. I could offer some tips and routines but it comes back to learning. Don't take what works for me, do some research and learn about foods that fit your body type, environment, lifestyle, and goals. Also, eat REAL food whenever possible. High quality meats, proteins, and vegetables (Ideally not the kind that you put in your freezer and microwave). It takes more time to prepare but these foods are what your body wants to get energy from. Also, let's all accept the fact that artificial sugar should be avoided entirely. There are documentaries and information available to you on the internet for more scientific evidence and data. In short, artificial sugars turn to fat. We all have cravings for sugary foods, mitigate those cravings as best you can. Learning about food and nutrition is fascinating and tracking your progress is very rewarding. You don't have to go overboard with it. Start small and gradually start to make the necessary changes that fit your life.

So, what happens now?

Now you understand that creating pull in your life will give you extra momentum to achieving your goals. You know that learning and searching for facts and knowledge is a time consuming but essential part of success. You also know some key areas that will drastically improve energy and wellbeing, exercise, education, and food. None of this matters if you don't take action. If you don't take action and get a gym membership right now then the chances of success decrease. If you don't start learning about health and nutrition right now, today, and so on then the chances of forming those habits decrease dramatically. A word of caution! You will fail and fall behind on some or maybe even all your goals the first time you try them. What do you do? Think about things that caused your failure, figure out how you can avoid those or make a task easier and then try again. Every time you practice or work you should be thinking, "How can I make this better?" "How can I do better this time around?" "What can I do to make this more efficient?" This process is easier than you think. Take a failure as a learning process. Take a failure and look at how incredible it was that you tried in the first place. Take a failure, dissect it and then go at it again.

Here is your blueprint.

1.) **Make sleep a priority**. Teenagers may need a couple more hours but current research says 6-7.5 hours per night is your target. Your sleep cycles take about 90 minutes each so ideally sleep for 6 or 7.5 so that you don't wake up in the middle of a cycle.
2.) **Exercise**. Even 20 minutes per day will increase your energy. Ideally, first thing in the morning when cortisol levels are high (cortisol is the stress hormone). Minimizing your stress hormone first thing in the morning is a great way to start every day.
3.) **Health and Nutrition**. Start adding more vegetables and high quality proteins into your meals. The fats from foods like avocado, almonds, and various nuts are excellent for energy and hormone regulation. ELIMINATE AS MUCH SUGAR FROM YOUR DIET AS POSSIBLE.
4.) **Define your goals**. Take some time to sit down and map out what you would like to accomplish in the next one, two, five, and ten years. If you are unsure about how to set goals I would suggest setting a few stretch goals and then add a few more goals that intimidate you but also inspire you. Remember, once you accomplish these goals you can set bigger goals, so get a few smaller successes and they will give you momentum for your larger goals.
5.) **Journaling**. Put the date and time and write for 20 minutes per day. You can write about events that

happened the day before, a funny moment you experienced, or your thoughts and feelings. I didn't enjoy journaling the first few times I tried it but it DOES help with well-being and achievement. Think about how valuable a journal of all your thoughts, ideas, and daily events will be in twenty or thirty years.

One last thing.

Your journey is going to be hard. Everyone has different goals so make sure to create your own. Go any direction so long as it is forward. I have adopted these strategies and routines from many different sources and I do not claim to be a certified professional. What I do know is that none of this matters if you don't take action. Start executing in all aspects of your life and you will get better at it every time. Execution can be something as simple as selling old things that you've "been meaning to get rid of" or it could be creating steps to starting a business that you've been thinking of. Send an email to someone in the field you want to pursue and ask them questions. Not only will you make the connection with that person but they will save you tons of time that would have been spent researching difficult questions. Make sure to respect others time and offer as much in return as you can. Here's how I used to get in contact with people. As of early 2017, video content is extremely valuable for businesses and marketing. I picked up a camera during college as a hobby and I realized how valuable this skill was. I started to email entrepreneurs in my area and offered to create and edit videos for them and in return I asked for their time and knowledge. This opened so many doors for me. I could create videos and photos for a business in a week and in return I would get all my questions answered! Many times, I would be working with someone and they would introduce me to someone else that I could talk to. Not only did I get priceless information but I built quality relationships with people and continue to collaborate with many of the people that I met. So, what can you do? Are you in great shape?

Many business people would love a free personal trainer. Do you know how to cook healthy meals? Offer to do meal prep or create a custom meal plan for someone who you want to meet. Get creative with this part of the process. There is no straight path to networking and finding mentors. Ask around and start to meet people, you will know who you want to learn from by the rapport you build with that person after a few meetings.

The future is unknown and times are moving rapidly. It seems like the moment we figure out one problem, two more appear. This will continue to happen, it's ok. It is your job to find what creates a fulfilling life for YOU. You will change this, as will I, so don't be afraid to pivot once you realize that your plan no longer works for you. To be honest, all this information could be out dated within the next five years. Until then, deliberately practice you craft, take action, ask great questions, and STOP WAITING FOR THE RIGHT TIME!

***

To contact Chad:

chadsteven@mail.com

Dr. Rhoda Lipscomb

Dr. Rhoda Lipscomb is a Positive Sexuality Specialist. She is an author and public speaker and has been counseling and consulting with individuals and couples in the area of human sexuality for over 25 years. She received her PhD in clinical sexology from the American Academy of Clinical Sexologists in Orlando, FL and her Masters of Science in Counseling from the University of Phoenix. She is an AASECT certified sex therapist with an ASCH certification in clinical hypnosis.

She specializes in the alternative sexuality communities, such as open relationships, GLBT, BDSM, ABDL, kink and fetishes. Her approach to therapy is helping people to understand, accept and appreciate their sexuality with all the wonderful unique flavors that come with it. Shame, embarrassment, guilt and fear are poisonous to healthy sexual expression so letting go of old, irrational and impractical belief patterns can pave the way for a new and exciting beginnings.

The Winds of Change Regarding Sexuality
By Rhoda J. Lipscomb, PhD

Sex and sexuality. Even the words can cause many in our Western society to immediately tense up. We have been taught to consider the mere mention of the subject taboo and a simple conversation of the subject in poor taste. Yet why? Sexuality starts when life starts. It is an innate part of the human condition, a part of every human's personality and what many feel is a sacred part of our birthright. So then, what is the big fuss all about?

Sex and sexuality are actually similar, yet different things. Sex relates to the specific sexual acts that human beings and animals engage in, either in pairs, groups or solo. Some of us think of sex as a simple act of physical pleasure, while for others it's a way of communicating deep feelings, and still others see sex as a spiritual experience. The definition of sexual activity also differs from person to person. (Siegel, 2011, p. xiii) There are a wide range of sexual activities that people enjoy and range from the very typical that most people are aware of, to some very unique and atypical behaviors. While there can be a great deal of shame and embarrassment about atypical sexual behaviors, so long as they are consented to by all involved, they are not bad, wrong or immoral; just different.

Sexuality is much more difficult to define. A search of several on-line dictionaries gives very different answers. Some talk about "attitudes" or "capacity for sexual feelings." Others confuse all of sexuality with sexual orientation, meaning whether one is sexually attracted to males, females or both. It has also been described as an expression of sexual interest and the attributes one is born with that only the individual themselves can truly understand and fully know. It is no wonder that the topic of sexuality is confusing when even the dictionaries cannot agree on a concise definition.

As someone with a doctoral degree in clinical sexology my professional experience has led me to understand the confusion. Sexuality is part of each individual's personality. It is part of what and who appeals to us sexually, how we react, even how we dress, talk, move and interact with others around us. It is beyond specific sexual behaviors and often runs deep in our souls. It is light and dark, giving and selfish, it can bring out our best and our worst, and it comforts us, excites us, frightens us, brings us together and tears us apart. No wonder we are so confused. Many of us wonder why others are so afraid of their sexualities and yet when we look at the power it commands, it is not really that surprising.

For people raised in Western culture, sexuality begins and thrives with fear, then becomes enhanced by misinformation, shame and embarrassment. There is also significant misunderstanding, enhanced by lack of accurate education about sex/sexuality and much of what we learn emerges from a negative, fear-based approach. Many adolescents grow up in homes with parents who do not talk about sex/sexuality, do not exhibit positive or healthy role-modeling, forcing adolescents to rely upon educational facilities that teach abstinence only education or the Internet. Children are only taught about body parts and reproduction with no mention of pleasure, excitement, arousal, or how to interact with a partner both emotionally and physically regarding sex. Parents, although uncomfortable discussing this subject with their children, many times strictly limit the amount and type of information the school systems are allowed to share and instruct.

In Western culture it is an acceptable form of thought that, in order to excel at an activity that there is a need to practice; whether it is sports, driving a car, cooking, playing a musical instrument, or any technical skill. Yet, many in this same demographic suggest that if a person practices their sexual skills they are a pervert, over-sexed, an addict, a slut, a whore or in need of counseling or a therapist. This shame permeates people's souls and greatly affects the way they interact with those they eventually form meaningful relationships and want to share their sexuality. While some people place the blame solely on religion, the shame is perpetuated by a large part of society that does not necessarily include people who are religious. The sexual shame, embarrassment and inhibition are rampant not because of religion but rather the judgment inflicted upon people in order to control the actions of society.

With a large segment of the population believing that this negative attitude about sex and sexuality is "normal" they are lulled into a false belief that all people share the same belief system. However, this is not true. Many people who were raised in European countries have a very different attitude about the subject viewing it as a natural part of life, nothing to get overly concerned about. Anthropologists show us that historically, there have been many cultures whose views regarding sex and sexuality more closely mirrored current European beliefs rather than those of the United States. Societies in which women have lots of autonomy and authority tend to be decidedly male-friendly, relaxed, tolerant, and plenty sexy. If you're a man and unhappy at the amount of sexual opportunity in your life, don't blame women. Instead, make sure they have equal access to power, wealth, and status. Then watch what happens. (Ryan & Jetha, 2010, p. 133-134) Of course, there are also cultures around the world with even more negative and repressive sexual attitudes especially when it comes to women and sexual minorities such as gay, lesbian and bisexual individuals.

Since there are many cultures with differing views and beliefs about sex and sexuality from very positive and open to very negative and repressive why should we even care how the beliefs and attitudes in our Western culture are the way they are? What affect do they have on us and those we care about? In the sections that follow we examine the ramifications.

Much of Western society's beliefs about sexuality are based on fear; fear of pregnancy, fear of sexually transmitted infections, fear of loss of one's reputation, fear of letting go, fear of getting hurt, and fear of public opinion. It affects the decisions we make about the relationships we choose, the reasons to stay in dysfunctional and unhealthy relationships that often keep people stuck because so many of us believe "that's just the way it is, the way it has always been and the way it is supposed to be." Yet this is not true.

Those who fear and hate sexuality (erotophobes) are attacking those who appreciate or tolerate sexuality (erotophiles). And while erotophiles are *not* attempting to force erotophobes to live more sexually adventurous lives, erotophobes insist that both sides—*everyone*—live according to their erotophobic values. (Klein, 2006, p. 1) We're being misled and misinformed by an unfounded yet constantly repeated mantra about the naturalness of wedded bliss, female sexual reticence, and happily-ever-after sexual monogamy—a narrative pitting man against woman in a tragic tango of unrealistic expectations, snowballing frustration, and crushing disappointment. Living under this tyranny of two, as author and media critic Laura Kipnis puts it, we carry the weight of "modern love's central anxiety," namely, the expectation that romance and sexual attraction can last a lifetime of coupled togetherness despite much hard evidence to the contrary. (Ryan & Jetha, 2010, p. 40-41)

These unrealistic/unattainable expectations lead people to make decisions based on fear rather than facts and to trust those who want to take advantage of those fears. This can include those who believe in the sex/porn addiction industry, which happens to be a fabricated diagnosis, solely for the purpose of making money off people's fear of their own sexuality. Sexual addiction is the latest tool of an antisex morality embedded in our culture at its deepest levels, labeling sexuality as dangerous evil temptation that must be constantly constrained and feared. (Ley, 2012, p. 211) Neither sex addiction nor porn addiction is listed in the DSM5 (Diagnostic and Statistical Manual of Mental Disorders, 5th edition) which is the manual used by mental health providers to diagnose mental illness.

This is a hotly debated issue within the sexological field, and while there is not enough room in this chapter for more on that topic, facts on why sex and porn addiction do not exist, can be found in the expert work of Marty Klein or David Ley.

This leads us to the main point of the change movement that has started in recent years, the movement towards positive sexuality. While as a researcher and academic I tend not to quote Wikipedia, however, their quote reflected a positive sexuality tone. Sex positivity is an attitude towards human sexuality that regards all consensual sexual activities as fundamentally healthy and pleasurable, and encourages sexual pleasure and experimentation. The sex-positive movement is a social and philosophical movement that advocates these attitudes. ("Sex-positive movement," 2016)

There is a growing movement of organizations and individuals especially within the field of sexology who are urging people to begin to examine and challenge their views about sexuality and allow more openness for everyone. The list includes the Center for Positive Sexuality, the Foundation for Sex Positive Culture, the Effing Foundation, the World Health Organization (WHO), and the International Society for Sexual Medicine and Planned Parenthood Federation among others.

While these organizations have mission statements describing their views on positive sexuality, the International Society for Sexual Medicine defines it as having positive attitudes about sex and feeling comfortable with one's own sexual identity and the sexual behaviors of others. They describe sex positive people as having the following traits:

Open to learning about sex, sexual activity, understanding their bodies as well as their partner's bodies as well as the emotional and psychological aspects involved in sexual intimacy

Understand the importance of safer sexual practices for both themselves and their partners. This includes physical safety, from unintended pregnancy and sexually transmitted infections, as well as emotional and psychological safety.

Believe sex is a healthy part of life that needs to be enjoyed and discussed without shame or awkwardness or as a taboo subject

Acknowledge that there are times when they and/or their partner are not in the mood for sexual activity

Accept others' sexual practices as long as the participants are consenting and feel safe without moral judgment even when others' behaviors are very different from their own (International Society for Sexual Medicine, n.d.)

Given this new body of information, we could conclude that the way people have looked at sexuality and relationships has been changing throughout time and it will continue to do so. Change is a force in our world that continues to happen and people have always found themselves in one of two camps; those who fear change and fight against it and those who embrace change and learn to adapt.

Erotophobes fear change in how we think about, talk about and express our sexuality. Their way of responding is to fight change by promoting fear and ignorance and reduce the options available for others to choose. Erotophiles want to embrace change, explore the various options and expand education and communication about sexuality for everyone to know what options are available and let others choose for themselves. It may seem like an "us against them" sort of mentality yet it need not be that way.

Given my professional experience, I have observed that people have sexual personality types. The mono-sexual type is comfortable and satisfied in an exclusive sexual relationship with one person for most, if not all of their life. The poly-sexual type needs more variety in their sexual relationships and this can exhibit itself in a wide variety of ways and styles. Then there are the adapter-sexual types who appear to be able to mold themselves to either of the other styles and have satisfying relationships of either style. It has been my professional experience that problems occur when a mono-sexual person and a poly-sexual person try to form a committed relationship since neither is comfortable with the others style.

Many from the mono-sexual style state that monogamy is the norm and is the foundation of a successful relationship. Yet if this were true, our society would not have such a high rate of divorce (which for decades has hovered around 50% and higher for second and third marriages) and infidelity (which vary from 40 to 70%). Data does not support the theory that monogamy guarantees happiness or stability in relationships. If a person were picking a stock or considering major surgery with a doctor who has such low success ratings, one might consider a new stock broker or a second option.

Make no mistake; the previous statements are not condemnation of those who want to pursue mono-sexual, exclusive sexual relationships. There can be many advantages to this style of relationship if both partners truly agree. However, this methodology clearly does not work for everyone. Food for thought and contemplation - in a country where we pride ourselves for our individual spirit, how did we come to fear being individuals and embrace conformity and mediocrity.

The world of positive sexuality embraces options for all; including the option of exclusive sexual relationships that are openly discussed, negotiated and agreed to rather than just assumed. Those in the monogamy world could learn and enhance their relationships greatly with more open communication about sexuality with their partner rather than less. As well as supporting their friends, family and neighbors who want to explore other sexuality options openly and freely without fear of disapproval or discrimination in employment, housing or divorce and child custody cases.

If a person has no interest in porn, going to a nude beach, or attending a swinger club, they are not forced to do so. Conversely, in order to support equality in positive sexuality, remove support from fear driven politicians and media, many of whom utilize their own freedoms, possibly out of their own shame and guilt, to take away the rights of others.

While it would be wonderful to wrap up this chapter on the change towards more positive sexuality in our culture and world with an easy concise answer to the problem, an issue with the depth and complexity of sexuality is not that easily packaged. Major change and shifts in perception, thinking and beliefs take time, contemplation and an energy shift to really take hold. The more we talk about options and alternatives to the typical negative sexual views of our Western culture, the more people realize there are other ways to think, feel, believe and behave as well as allow others to choose to live their sexual lives. A healthier approach would be to throw out the outdated vision of "how it should be," because this keeps one trapped in fantasy. Instead allow your love, sexuality, and relational life to take on alternative and creative frameworks, meanings, configurations, and trajectories. (Donaghue, 2015, p. 193-194)

As a TV commercial for the Dove brand of chocolate states, live each day as if it is your only one. Choose pleasure! (*Dove brand chocolate*, 2017) Let's make choosing pleasure more about the pleasure of our bodies and minds rather than items filled with excess sugar and preservatives. Let's choose positive sexual pleasure for everyone who wants it.

***

To contact Rhoda:

www.drrhoda.com

drrhoda@yahoo.com

720-530-6545

References

Choose pleasure [Advertisement]. (2017). unknown: .

Donaghue, C. (2015). *Sex outside the lines*. Dallas, TX: Benbella Books.

International Society for Sexual Medicine. (n.d.). www.issm.info/sexual-health-qu/what-does-sex-positive-mean

Klein, M. (2006). *America's war on sex*. Westport, CT: Praeger Publishers.

Ley, D. J. (2012). *The myth of sex addiction*. Lanham, Maryland: Rowman & Littlefield.

Ryan, C., & Jetha, C. (2010). *Sex at Dawn: How we mate, why we stray, and what it means for modern relationships*. New York: Harper.

Sex-positive movement. (2016). In *Sex-positive movement*. Retrieved January 7, 2017, from https//en.wikipedia.org/wiki/sex-positive_movement

Siegel, S. (2011). *Your brain on sex: How smarter sex can change your life*. Naperville, IL: Sourcebooks.

Dr. LeAnne N. Smith

Dr. LeAnne N. Smith was an immigrant from Vietnam. In 1975, when she was 11 years old together with her mother and two brothers escaped Vietnam to come to America.

Most of Dr. Smith's education took place here in America, UCSD, SDSU and Huntington Pacific College. She obtained a Ph.D. in Psychology with an emphasis in Behavior Science in 2005.

Dr. Smith is a High-Performance Coach, Business Strategist, and an independent Public Relation & Marketer.

Dr. LeAnne Smith is also National Sales Trainer with Eric Lofholm International, a global sales training organization. She offers a comprehensive training experience through a variety of deliverables including one-time pieces of training or repeat sessions to build company-wide skill sets.

Dr. Smith's number one passion is to share life strategies with men and women of all ages on how to live **"Life by Design"**. Dr. Smith's coaching approach inspired men and women on how to monetize their passions through self-belief and unwavering mindset.

Dr. LeAnne Smith is a Mom of two, an avid learner, a Certified College Funding, and a Momentum Forex trader. When she is not spending time with her family, Dr. Smith is an advocate and supporter of Stop Child Abuse; Single Parent Association of America; Save The Children; and the Young Heroes Scholarship Foundation.

The Art of Being F.A.K.E.
The Secrets to the Mastery of Self-Actualization
By Dr. LeAnne N. Smith

I came to America in 1975, as an immigrant from Vietnam. I was 12 years old. There were few American Phrases I learned and liked when I first came to America such as:

"As Easy as Pie"

"Bigger Bang for your Buck"

"Between a Rock and a Hard Place"

Over the years, I learned to appreciate the truism of the American Phrase **"You have to FAKE until you MAKE it"**. This philosophy helped me survive in the highly competitive world of business as well as personal development arena.

For a while, there, even though when FAKING it had everyone around me believed in my ability and competency as a business owner, and an entrepreneur, deep down inside I know I am indeed just FAKING it! Although I know fully well within myself that it was necessary to put up a strong and competent "FAKING it" face in order to buy myself time, to learn, to perfect my skill set, and build the confidence I needed to propel forward in my career as a first entrepreneur in my family in America. Nevertheless, I resent the negative connotation behind the word "FAKE". I also often wondered, will I know when my FAKING become MAKING it. Will it be a smooth, seamless transition? Will people know or be aware of my transition from being FAKE to MAKING it into reality?

Needless to say, I was uncomfortable and full of mixed feelings between the appreciations for the concept of "You have to FAKE it until you MAKE it" and resenting it at the same time.

While I was struggling with my mixed feelings, one of my favorite quotes surfaced,

"Whatever makes you uncomfortable is your Biggest opportunity for Growth"

Bryant McGill.

McGill's philosophy helped me realized that unless it's brain surgery, I have the power to question, to change, and manage my own thoughts. Correct mindsets directly affect my actions or reaction to circumstances for the betterment of myself and others around me.

In order to bring forth a positive spin to the phrase "You have to FAKE it until you MAKE it", I came up with an acronym F.A.K.E.

F: Flexible

A: Ask for Help

K: Know Your Own Worth

E: Evaluate

F - Be Flexible

"Empty your mind, be formless. Shapeless, like water."

Bruce Lee

When we meet resistance, go deep or better yet, go around it. When the river meets an obstacle, it follows the path of least resistance – by flowing around it. Often than not, we seem to reach dead ends, not necessarily because the challenges are too great for us to overcome, but rather we are not flexible in our thinking. We do not always have to meet every challenge and obstacle "head on." We too can be flexible and bendable like the river. Choose the path of "least resistance". It could very well be our best strategy yet!

We would rather be right than to be open minded and take the risks trying new approaches to deal with our challenges. The only thing that will never change is that everything is changing. We cannot get to our success until we learn to accept changes and grow with it.

Imagine the obstacle in your path is a large log that has deeply rooted itself in the river bed. You are just doing your thing, everything flowing into your life is just beautiful and perfect…until you run into the challenge/obstacle logs that you cannot seem to get your arms around them. You have to choose, either get out the biggest chainsaw and cut your way out to your end goals, or you can collectively and strategically flow your way "around" the obstacle. This is not by any means ignoring that fact the challenges are real, and they are on your path to success. What it means is that you choose to be flexible and be open-minded trying new approaches to deal with this log of obstacles. For every new challenge and obstacle, there are new innovative ways to successfully deal with them. Be wise, and choose the path of "least resistance".

"What matters most is how well you walk through the fire"

Charles Bukowski

"Circumstances are the rulers of the weak; they are instruments of the wise."

Samuel Lover

A - Ask for Help

"He who sees a need and waits to be asked for help is as unkind as if he had refused it." - Dante Alighieri

Do not be afraid to ask for help. When you ask for input from others, you will increase your options for resolutions.

This is when your choice of friends and supporters play an important role in lending their expertise and constructive support. At times, step outside of your circle of friends and step into the realm of professional help.

> *"First-rate people hire first-rate people; second-rate people hire third-rate people." - Leo Rosten*
>
> *"I don't want any yes-men around me. I want everybody to tell me the truth, even if it costs them their jobs.Samuel Goldwyn*

K - Know Your Worth

"The key to Immortality is first living a life worth remembering"

Bruce Lee

Know that you are God's creation. To put yourself down is to put down the very thing God that created you for. How I work toward dealing with my own fears of failure is to know my **W.O.R.T.H.**

W – Will yourself to self-discipline. Success is a habit. Habit can be learned by repetition. It takes self-discipline to put yourself through daily repetition of behaviors and beliefs that help you choose to dominate your fears.

O – Organize our priorities in order to succeed. We may be doing too much or taking on excessive tasks that would prevent us from fulfilling our life's prophecy. We often have excuses about not having enough time in a day to do everything we want to accomplish. It's not about time management, but rather Self-Management. Organize your priorities to match your goals and you will effectively get where you want to be.

R –Ride Out life's Ups and Downs. We are at times our worst critics and punishers. Living Life is a process, and within that process, we are exposed to a wide range of experiences and feelings – good, bad or indifferent. While in the midst of living our lives, we often find it difficult to see beyond the black and white. We fail to see the rainbows at the end of every storm. We need to accept all that we are, and all that we can do. The only way we can enjoy the wave of life is to have the courage to get on, ride it, AND have the ability to stay on top. To do that, we need to learn how to ride the waves of our ups and downs of life. We need to stop being so hard on ourselves and learn techniques not to fall off. And if you do, retake that very first step again – by getting back on, again, and again. So take heart, and take it easy on yourself.

"Doing the best at this moment puts you in the best place for the next moment"

Oprah Winfrey

T - Test Out your problem-solving theories. I came up with six steps for reaching

      1. **Identify the obstacles surrounding the problem** by identifying what issue is becoming a conflict. Stop the process and address the issue and then collect yourself and address the issue from the proper perspective – that of resolution.

"If you can't state your problem in ten words or less – you don't understand it yourself"

R.G. Campbell

"You shouldn't take the fence down until you know the reason why it was up"

G.K. Chesteron

2. **Identify the party/parties involved (the stakeholders)**. It's equally important to identify the parties involved in finding the solution itself. More importantly, attack the issue and not the person.

"Never fight too often with one enemy or you will teach him your art of war"

Sir Arthur Helps

3. **Identify the interests of the stakeholders.** By finding out where the conflict comes from and the people that are involved, you then can better navigate, plan and get cooperation from all that are involved.

It's important to realize that people have different objectives, goals, needs and values. People also have different perceptions, motives, actions and words. The ability to identify the interests of each person involved, individually and collectively, will provide a better chance to create winners, address all the interests, and establish ground rules – ones which seek common ground.

4. **Brainstorm options.** Since people have different expectations as to what is a favorable outcome, it is imperative that you involve all the stakeholders in the solution process. There is a great need to create ownership with everyone involved so they can have a safe place to participate in finding the solution to the problem or conflicts.

5. **Evaluate options.** In evaluating options, keep in mind that conflict that is not resolved can become unhealthy; it can create a win/lose situation.

6. **Choose wisely.** Choose solution(s) that solve the problem and meet the interest of the stakeholders using objective standards that are wise and fair.

H - Honor yourself though celebrations. Rewarding yourself as you go is a way to motivate yourself. It is important to recognize your achievement by celebrating it. Your reward does not have to be something extravagant or elaborate. It could be a simple day of rest, a walk on the beach, a day of beauty, or a trip to your favorite restaurant and a movie afterward. These little rewards will keep you motivated and focused on achieving your goals.

E - Evaluate your Self-Esteem

"The Equation for Self-Love comes from Self-Forgiveness plus Self-Acceptance"

Dr LeAnne N. Smith

The definition of **Esteem** is to place a high value on; to respect; to be considered favorable; to consider valuable.

Work on your Self-Esteem. This is where you see many overnight movie stars and millionaires find themselves in trouble either with the law, personal relationships or both. Many of them fall as fast as they rose. What are some reasons for this turbulent path?

I would take a calculated risk and say, perhaps it is all due to their fear of success. Our whole being (mind, body, and soul) and purpose are to keep ourselves in a homeostasis state at all times. With the mind being the captain, the hard drive of the entire body, whatever it believes and wants, the rest of the body follows.

When we are feeling worthlessness and inadequate, or feeling that we somehow do not deserve success, it may be due to a fear of success. One of my favorite quotes that I often think of whenever I feel afraid is

"Courage is not having lack of fear, but rather the mastery of it"

Mark Twain

Instead of caving into our fears, let's find ways to master them. One step I am going to suggest for dealing with the fear of success is to evaluate on your self-esteem and do this often.

Self-esteem is about how we view our own self. Do we place ourselves in high value? Do we respect ourselves? Do we consider ourselves to be favorable within ourselves and among people around us? Do we consider ourselves valuable? Unfortunately, some of us often admire others and do not spend enough time acknowledging ourselves. In doing so, we give admirations and favorable considerations to others and not to our own accomplishments.

"If you think you're too small to be effective, you have never been in bed with a mosquito"

Bette Reese

Your Story Becomes YOU

"Every theory is a self-fulfilling prophecy that orders experience into the framework it provides"

Ruth Hubbard

Unfortunately, we often value and respect the success of others more than our own. It's about time we take charge and be our own promoters and "raving" fans. Be proactive and responsible for your own intrinsic and extrinsic source of encouragement system.

Surround yourself with positive affirmations. Envision yourself at the end of your journey to success. See it, feel it, smell it, touch it! Make it **REAL!** Every day and every way, make it known to yourself, and everyone around you, you are getting closer and closer to living your dream. The dream that was designed **by YOU,** and **for YOU**.

Surround yourself with people that are not only positive to be around but also have the vision, the passion and the drive with their own goals. Above all, surround yourself with people who know first-hand what it takes to focus and persevere in order to succeed. These are the people that would gladly and generously help you on your way to your own success.

Envision yourself at get together with some great friends. Everyone around you is positive and successful. Not only in their own personal lives but also professionally (can't have one without the other).

You are among friends, and there is never a shortage of words of encouragement and sincere caring for each other. The general motto of this special group of friends is "How can I be a source of help or of encouragement in your life?"

These are the people that genuinely want to see you succeed. These are the people who are willingly going out of their way to be a source of enhancement in your life.

'It's better to known by six people for something you're proud of than by six million for something you are not"

Albert Brooks

"No One can make you feel inferior without your consent"

Eleanor Roosevelt

"Associate with men of good quality if you esteem your own reputation; for it is better to be alone than in bad company."

George Washington

Therefore, choose wisely the things you say to yourself. More importantly, chose your friends wisely.

Focus & Concentration

"It is during our darkest moments that we must focus to see the light"

Aristotle Onassis

Be consistent in adding fuel to your ability to focus

When the going gets tough, the tough get going. It is certainly easier said than done. We often allow obstacles and challenges to hinder the goal we set. It is very easy to plow through the everyday grind of hurdles and challenges and lose focus of the original goal of our effort, our passion, and our commitment.

When we take our eyes off the focus of our goal, our goal is no longer the focus of our attention and intention. Do not allow obstacles to get the best of you. Do not wait until you are worn out. Be consistent in adding fuel to your ability to focus. How do we add fuel to our ability to keep our focus? You can accomplish this by practicing the following steps.

Make a conscious habit of reminding ourselves of our goal every day.

When the going gets rough, take a few moments and **B.R.E.A.T.H.**

Believe in yourself

Reconfirm your commitment

Evaluate your current plan of action

Affirm your passion for success

Timing is everything

Hope is having faith in your own ability and instinct.

"There is a difference between interest and commitment. When you're interested in doing something, you do it when it's convenient. When you're committed to something, you accept no excuses; only results."

Kenneth Blanchard

Be Still

"The Art of enjoying life journey is a personal matter. It's made up of moments of contemplation, silence and abstraction"

Dr LeAnne N. Smith

Feeling stuck? Backtrack your steps. Most often, the best decision is not to have one. Whenever you're facing challenges or unfamiliar territory, step back, give yourself space and time to be still. Do not be rattled by the sounds of nearby troubles, rather, be forever more attentive to your own voice of reason; re-confirming your WHY's, for in the midst of stillness, comes the ingenious sound of intuition.

"Sometimes the best deals are the ones you don't make"

Bill Veeck

"A man of high ambitions must leave even his fellow adventures and go forth into deeper solitude and greater trials"

Author Unknown

"Let us never confuse stability with stagnation"

Mary Jean LeTendre

Learn to Laugh at Yourself

"Success isn't final. Failure isn't fatal

It would be challenging to be enthusiastic about life when we are in constant turmoil about our own failures and shortcomings. To overcome this challenge, we need to acquire the skills of taking things in life lightly.

Learn to laugh at ourselves. The ability to make fun of ourselves will give us the ability to accept our own humanistic frailties.

Self-acceptance gives us the ability to forgive ourselves. This is an important process that each of us must master, for without enthusiasm and humor, we will not survive long in the race of excellence. Being human is to fail at times, and that is part of life's journey. Success is a process and not a destiny.

Live your best every day. Accept what you CAN do and surrender to things that you have control over.

Forget **"Perfection."** Perfection is the twin sister of "Fear of Failure." We all have heard it before, "If I cannot do it perfectly, then I do not want to do it at all." It is certainly an excuse, but it works! This mindset helps us justify why we do not want to start things that we know would help us succeed in the long run.

"It is doubtful if anyone ever made a success of something that waited until ALL the conditions were just right before starting" - *Anonymous*

Therefore, forget about "PERFECTION." It is harmful to your winning mindset and damping your success.

Forgive Yourself

"If you wish to travel far and fast, travel light. Take off all our envies, jealousies, unforgiveness, selfishness and fears.

Glenn Clark

Most often it's easier for us to forgive friends, family members and even people we do not know who wronged and disappointed us. Yet, the very person we may have the most trouble forgiving is ourselves.

To not forgive is not to forget. Until we forget our shortcomings, our disappointments, and all the negative feelings that are associated with our failures, we have a tendency to go back and dwell on the past. This is not about forgetting the lesson learned but to do better the next time around. This is about self-defeating mindsets and negative thinking such as: what could have been; what you could have done better; why did you not see it coming; I was such a fool, etc. **Life waits for no-one. Let's forget about it and move on!**

***

To contact LeAnne:

www.MindsetOfChampions.org

888.727.4979

drLeAnneNSmith@gmail.com

Angela Barrows

Angela Barrows is The Empowerment Coach, considered by many to be a leading expert in personal empowerment and spiritual development. She commands many an audience with her channeled and inspirational presentations in New Zealand, Australia, the UK and USA. Online and via her popular workshops and programs for teens and adults, she assists clients of all ages from all over the world to live an empowered life.

If you're scared of doing something that's really important for you because you feel powerless and lack confidence in yourself and your abilities, remember that personal empowerment is a choice.

You can choose to be disempowered or you can choose to be empowered. You have a choice to work hard, to unleash your freedom and to give yourself and family the best possible future. You have a choice, so stop struggling and Be Personally Empowered!

You Have a Choice. So Choose to Stop Struggling
By Angela Barrows

We have all had times when we haven't been or felt empowered. Times when we haven't had the confidence that we felt we needed, and therefore, struggled through issues in our life. So many of us consider it to be 'normal' to travel through life feeling frustrated and not able to feel connected to others. Is this something you're familiar with?

I used to find it difficult to communicate what I wanted and needed from others. This lead to me becoming more frustrated with things in my life not going well or how I had planned.

Often feeling lonely and not accepted socially into a group, I felt angry at the world for not understanding me. I frequently felt overwhelmed due to the expectations of society and how I was expected to behave. I was fed up with constantly feeling fed up, disempowered, and under-valued as a person.

Unfortunately, it was a long time before I realized that *I* didn't value, accept, or love myself as a person. So how could I expect that of others?

I wanted to feel empowered in any situation: work, relationships or with my friends and immediate family and I was desperate to be 'normal' like others appeared to be. However, I was always afraid to communicate what was going on for me in case I didn't feel heard. So I never felt heard.

That was my motivation to eventually create my unique Empowerment programs, to help others break down *their* perceived barriers so they also can move through *their* fears. To enable them to rebuild their self-confidence, and experience an enhanced connection with themselves and others as I did.

This reminds me of a story of a young woman who was born with two holes in her heart. This was a serious heart condition which caused her to die a few times, immediately after she was born. Still in hospital several months later, they were unsure if she was going to live and for how long. Her worried parents were told that if she was lucky, she may live to be 16 years of age.

Along with this, she was born with a lazy eye. This caused a great deal of consternation and embarrassment due to ongoing correction methods which included eye patches and thick lens corrective glasses. As you can imagine, she was teased incessantly! 'Bug eye', 'bung eye' the name calling was non-stop and she was frequently at the butt of cruel pranks by other children.

Already feeling different, she had trouble pronouncing words and speaking clearly. The private school which she attended sent her to weekly speech therapy lessons in the hope she would be restored to 'normal' and catch up with the rest of the class. It wasn't until she was 15, that the education system picked up that she was dyslexic.

For many years she was bullied and teased for the smallest of things. These things she had to learn to live with, yet back then, they contributed to her ongoing feeling of disempowerment.

She tells stories of being a young 8-year-old girl attending a Christian girl's youth group. There was this one girl there who would always tease her, calling her all sorts of names: bung eye and lazy eye, amongst others. Although her older sister was there and would stick up for her, she herself, wanted to have the courage to stand up for herself instead of running away, hiding and crying.

She lost count of the amount of times she was bullied for having a lazy eye, teased for not being able to speak properly, and teased again, for rarely being able to give the correct answers in class.

The torturous years spent in a private Catholic High school were a never ending experience of shame and embarrassment. Especially during class assignments which involved preparing and delivering a speech. She refused to ever do a speech because she was too scared to get up in front of her classmates and present, even though she had known them her whole school life.

She refused because she didn't want to fail by embarrassing herself, yet ended up failing the exam through not participating.

When I was growing up, I wanted to stand up for myself too. Like so many other children who must endure being constantly bullied, I hoped they would eventually find someone else to pick on and leave me alone. Although it was mainly name calling, being left out of the group and feeling alone used to really bother me. I was astounded to later experience corporate bullying from a large corporation in my adult years.

Even though adult bullying takes a different form, it's still unnerving to be on the receiving end.

As a young girl, I wanted to fight back. I wanted them to know how it feels to be on the other side. Thank goodness my father stepped in. Dad was a previous flyweight boxing champion and wanted his girls to be strong and able to defend themselves.

This was the beginning of my journey into martial arts. When I was 10 years old, I had my first karate competition fight. As I stood there in the square, feeling like was I invincible and waiting for the command to start my first competitive fight, I looked up at my mother who was watching from upstairs and she smiled. I felt so lucky to have two supportive parents to support my u I was ready to fight this girl and impress them with my new found skills. I thought of all those girls who had bullied me and I fought with everything I had in me.

Competitive fighting became a passion which eventually led to competing at National level in Taekwondo, then later in competitive boxing. I trained and participated in National Level competitions! However, after suffering through numerous boxing related injuries, I decided that the injuries were becoming too frequent and debilitating, so I stepped back from the elite level of competition Taekwondo.

It had taken a while, but now I was fighting for what was right for *me*. No longer having the need to prove my ability to defend myself, I made the decision to stop making myself feel disempowered by making bad decisions, and instead, to fight for what I most wanted in my life.

I decided to figure out how to live an empowered life, to feel strong in myself, to accept The Good the Bad and the Ugly. I wanted to take on the world and lead a global movement, to be and feel accepted and to feel like we all belong. I wanted to achieve my dream to achieve those goals which I could see so clearly. Most of all, I wanted to truly believe in myself.

Do you want to continue being the person who doesn't feel heard, who lacks confidence, and doesn't hold their own sense of power? Do you want to keep feeling powerless, as though someone or something else is controlling your life?

Maybe you feel that people just don't understand you and that you don't fit in, or that others are better than you? Or feel that you have goals and dreams that you can't achieve because you don't know how to communicate them? Do you feel that people will laugh at you for having those dreams? Do you hide away and feel lonely and anxious and overwhelmed at the thought of being around people? Does having to communicate and speak up for what you want and need feel overwhelming a lot of the time?

This is how I thought and felt when I was younger. Because of this I went inside myself and became introverted. In my mind I started to tell myself all sorts of lies such as: I'm not good enough, why would anyone listen to *me*?

But *I* was listening to me as I repeated these convincing statements: I'm not like my brother and sisters, I'm sure I'm adopted, I'm not beautiful like them, I feel like the ugly duckling, I don't get treated the same as my brother and sisters and so on. I would frequently compare myself to them. It wasn't until later in life that I realized I was treated the same (and better) due to some challenges I had faced.

I have always been a fan of personal development, my favorites are Tony Robbins, Zig Ziglar, Dale Carnegie - all the personal development legends. I would listen to them time and time again back in the day on tapes while driving in my car, listening to their words of wisdom. I wanted to be like them, I wanted to be empowered and wanted to help support and guide others to become empowered and to reach their dreams.

So I started *my* quest to become personally empowered.

In 2006 at 26 years of age, I left New Zealand to embark on what was going to be an amazing adventure of two young female friends backpacking around Europe. One of my biggest breakthroughs was to leave New Zealand! As we left the realization hit that OMG I am leaving my comfort zone for the next six months?!

We adjusted to a new way of life as we travelled around backpacking from place to place, meeting new people.

Six months later, while sitting on the beach with the sun beaming down on me and reading a book in the Greek Islands, I decided that I was *not* going to return home to my corporate job and my old life. There was *no way* I could go back to being in an unfulfilled space and carry on as before. I wanted to continue adventuring on, outside of my comfort zone!

I made the decision right there and then to move to the UK, to London. This was a frightening thought, as all I had was a backpack and the clothes that I had on my back *and* my money was running out. On my travels I was lucky to have met a new friend, and we decided to flat together.

Settling into London life as much as I could, I found a great corporate job and met some great people.

However, being back in the corporate world wasn't what my soul wanted to do! My soul yearned to be a Coach and a Guide, to support humanity like the masters who had so inspired me.

I wanted to become an inspirational speaker on Personal Empowerment.

So, I decided to have a YES year and to have the best year ever! It's amazing how life really begins when you decide to take on every opportunity which is presented to you!

Well! Having made that decision, *I* said YES to moving to Turkey and becoming a tour guide, to go and speak on a bus load of 30-49 people touring all around Turkey and Greece! What am I doing? I thought to myself. I'm actually *going*? But I don't like to speak in big groups!

Yet I had decided to say yes, to step out of my comfort zone and not let *anything* hold me back from stepping into my personal power. As I look back today, it is amazing how I continued to break through my fears after making that one decision.

I met some amazing people, saw some outrageous historical sites and had the best time of my life. It was a year of breakthrough. It was a year of not knowing what was around the corner. Of having to manage difficult situations while being in a foreign country where women aren't respected. Being a single blonde female in that situation was difficult but I managed.

It taught me a lot about people of all different cultures. Most importantly it showed me what I am capable of... And how being empowered the whole time, was simply inside of me, waiting to be led out.

After my adventure around Turkey I moved back to the UK, back to London to move back into the corporate world. I figured I had my gap year and now it was time to get serious with my life. As I arrived back in the big smoke it seemed so foreign to me and my soul was not happy. I found myself thinking what am I doing here? Where else can I go? What should I do? So after all that LIFE I have just experienced, I'm returning to the *corporate world* again?

My soul was not singing at that thought.

I decided I needed another challenge. This time I decided to move to Vietnam and be a tour guide in a country where not many people spoke English. My soul was still longing for a place to belong, longing for home, longing for a place where I felt I was respected and appreciated.

Once again I met the most amazing passengers on my tours around Vietnam, Cambodia, Laos China, and Thailand. I also did *blind* tours. Blind tours are when you have never previously been to a country and you're expected to lead your tour group - even though this is your first visit as well! This was waaay out of my comfort zone, yet I did it!

One of my dreams was to have my 30th birthday on the Great Wall of China and this happened!

I felt overwhelming emotions again and again along the journey when seeing the tragedies of War, poverty and corruption. As we drove past homeless women, children and complete families on the streets and in shacks, I often looked back and was thankful for what I had in my own life. Thankful that I had the choice to stay where I was or to move to a better place, that I had the option and the ability to do.

On my way home back to New Zealand in 2010, I made a promise to myself:

This is it. You're going to live your purpose, to Spiritually Inspire and Personally Empower others to live and enjoy an inspired and empowered life!

Utilizing the unique gifts, I had been born with, I started teaching spiritual development classes, co-developing breakthrough techniques and personal empowerment practices. I began speaking at spiritual centers and studied to become an NLP trainer, and learnt other modalities which I could use to help people break through their self-imposed limitations.

I then developed my two breakthrough signature programs:

The principles of Spiritually Inspired are to learn unique tools and techniques to expand your conscious awareness and vibration levels. This breakthrough program teaches you how to manage emotions (and the triggers) so you can choose *how* to respond in any given situation. This enables you to become empowered in your everyday life, which then enables you to live to your higher purpose.

By aligning your human points into your soul points (these are different to chakras) we bring your emotional, spiritual and mental aspects together and into harmony. This enables you to push through fears which have held you back from enjoying mental stability and clarity of mind. It also restores your creativity and gives you the ability to create your own emotional balance and peace.

The concept of Be Personally Empowered! is to engage you to empower yourself instead of waiting for others to empower you. Know how to stand tall and be proud of yourself moving forward.

We do this by uncovering all the lies (the limiting beliefs) you're telling yourself, removing the lies and reprogramming the lies so you can discover a truth about yourself which is more productive and has a positive impact on your life. This can all be achieved as you begin to understand, accept and embrace your challenges.

Along the way you will discover why your life isn't working the way you want it to and become clear on what is really important for you (your personal values.) We open up communication with your heart so you can manage those emotions, then we manage your mind so your mind can create and think clearly. We then connect these to your gut to support you and keep you stable as you bring alignment and congruency *consistently* into your life.

These are not magical methods which change you overnight. This is a simple yet profound step by step process which you can use to move forward more positively in your life and is the key to achieving personal empowerment. It's the most *essential* step you can take forward to personally empower your life!

Do you remember the little girl I was telling you about? Did I mention that young woman was me?

I still have two holes in my heart and have well exceeded my doctors' expectations. I competed in high level competitive martial arts, travelled extensively and still to this day am much fitter than the average person.

I remain a mystery to the medical team, who still want to do tests so they can marvel at the miracle I am, still have a lazy eye and minor speech impediments which you wouldn't realize when conversing with me. And yes I'm still dyslexic (thank you Jacqui and spell-check!)

This young lady grew up and eventually accepted her downfalls. She now embraces all the challenges which come her way and nothing stops her, she puts every effort into achieving her ideal outcome.

She chooses to live an empowered life, and has done things which not many people would have the guts and the courage to do. She faces her fears and overcomes her fears, steps out and brightens up many lives today. As you can too.

***

To contact Angela:

Check out her revolutionary methods to empower your life today:

Website: www.theempowermentcoach.com

Email: angela@theempowermentcoach.com

Facebook: www.facebook.com/TheEmpowermentCoach/

Skype: angelatheempowermentcoach

Founder and Host of The Empowerment Show, real people sharing knowledge, wisdom and stories of personal empowerment. Tune in here: www.theempowermentshow.com

Facebook: www.facebook.com/TheEmpowermentShowOnline/

Casandra Carmine

Casandra Carmine, was born in Meridian, Miss. but didn't spend much time there. She has lived all around the US. She also, spent four years in majestic Garmisch, Germany with her five children and now former husband, as a Military Wife.

Casandra has a diversified background including the arts, and in the technology field, as an Analyst for Jansen as a Contractor, and a Field Energy Consultant for Solar City.

She has a myriad of experience in training and management development, public speaking, and international travel. Casandra especially enjoyed the vibrant colors and the cultural experiences that India, the Philippines, and South America provided.

She served as a Volunteer for the VA Medical Center, in Salt Lake City, by leading Art Therapy groups for an inpatient psychiatry program. Her experiences while helping veterans provided Casandra with lessons in understanding, patience and empathy for others.

All of Casandra's vast experiences have brought her to a keener sense of self-actualization.

She sees and appreciates all the beauty around her. Casandra has trained herself to find new perspectives in everything she sees and does. Her **VISION,** since childhood, has always been to Touch, Move and Inspire those that she meets, always wanting to leave a note of positivity.

Take a Step Left, Victim to Victor

By Casandra Carmine

It was 1973, and as I opened my midterm report card, I stared at it in disbelief.

How could I get a C, in Mr. Curry's English writing class, when all my papers were A's?

This is obviously a mistake I thought to myself. So I marched to his class, all ready to stand my ground with him.

As I walked into his classroom, Mr. Curry was at his desk and looked up, he said "Hello Sandy, what can I do for you?"

I said, "Well first, how can I get a C on my report card, when all my grades in your class are A's?"

He said, "Let's talk after school." I looked at him skeptically and said, "Well I can't talk after school." I knew I had to be to work, but he didn't know that.

He told me, "If this is important to you, you will be here after school."

So begrudgingly, I said, "I will see you after school,"

He said, "Good, don't be late, like you are to my class every day."

As I was leaving, I was in a state of panic and distress. I had to work, and I couldn't miss work, as I was on my own supporting myself, and I had bills to pay. I called my boss and told him I would be late for work. I asked if I could make up the time over the weekend. My boss was shocked and concerned, as I was never late, and he wanted to know what was wrong. I explained I had to see my teacher, and he responded, "Let's talk when you get here tonight and no worries."

At the end of the day I hurried back to Mr. Curry's classroom, and found him waiting for me.

He said "You're not late, it's a miracle. Ok then let's talk"

I said "Mr. Curry how can you justify giving me a C, when all my grades are A's?"

He looked at me, intensely, and the silence seemed like it would never end. I couldn't take it anymore. It was like a staring contest with no end. Finally, I broke the silence with, "Well, Why?"

Mr. Curry looked at me calmly and sternly said "You are always late to my class."

I just looked at him and said, "Ok, so what's that got to do with my grades and my writing in this class? Which you always write excellent on."

He replied, "Everything" I thought. Everything?

"Sandy", he asked, "Do you have an after-school job?"

I was silent, how could I tell him, of course I had a job, I am on my own. The truth was he didn't know that, no teacher in school did, only my friends.

Sick of the silence, I said "Mr. Curry, I work after school, I have to, I am on my own."

He said "So, you're sounding like a victim, are you?"

I said "Of course not", he said "That's how you sound." I said "I am not a victim of anything."

He said "Say it again, with passion and substance." So, I did. Again, I said "I am not a Victim."

He said "Really?" I said "Of course not."

He said, "Then mean what you say."

He asked, "Do you drive the same way to school every day?"

I said "Yes, it's the fastest route, and what does that have to do with being called a victim?"

He said, "I want you to pick a different route when you drive to school tomorrow, you will see new things, a fresh perspective."

Mr. Curry said, "There is so much out there in life, so many things to see and experience, I understand and commend you for staying in school. But, you must stop being late to my class, and right now, school is your career, and then it will take you to your next career. "

He said "It goes again to the perspective you give it, a class or your career. Take a new perspective on everything." "A VICTIM or a VICTOR"

He asked me, "If a tidal wave was coming at you would you stand there or move out of the way? "

I looked at him, and said "Of course I would move out of the way."

He said, "Well, your C is your tidal wave, so what are you going to do? Are you going to stand there, or take a step left and change your outcome?"

I said, "I am going to take a step left and be on time to your class and change it, and you will see."

He said, "Oh Really"

The next day, I drove to school a different way, really trying to see the world around me, and what was out there, taking time to really see and not just look.

I have taken that philosophy with me in everything I have done after that meeting.

I am a Victor not a Victim, and though I was on my own in High School, I was going to graduate and go to College. On graduation day, my name was called, and as I walked across the stage, to receive my diploma to my surprise, I heard my name being announced for a scholarship.

I was in shock, but delighted, I was really going to College!

Until that conversation with Mr. Curry, I didn't even think I was going to graduate High School, and here I was walking across the stage a Victor! I looked out in the audience, and I could see my father, an Italian Immigrant, who barely finished the 6th grade, but worked so hard his whole life, looking up at me with joy. He had worked so hard to get me to this point.

I was going to College, because I was a Victor. I took the steps to succeed, changing my perspective, day after day, as Mr. Curry's voice rang through my whole being. Taking a step left, driving a new perspective changed my outcome.

I have chosen that in my life, in all I have done since then. As the many mountains and many valleys I have walked, I have often stepped left. Many doors have closed, but new ones have always opened. And if a door wouldn't open, then I would knock it down, or find a new way to achieve what I set out to do.

There is that adage we have heard over and over, attitude is everything, but it's also our actions and reactions that we choose in situations that are thrown at us. It is our choice: Are we a Victim or do we choose to be a Victor?

As a baby, we usually crawl first and then try to walk. We keep going, crawling again, and again. Trying different moves, we get up and keep going, we don't think about falling, or failing we just do. We try and do, with a different perspective. Not even thinking about it, just doing it.

You must first have a Vision. What is it you are passionate about?

STEPS to SUPPORT YOU IN YOUR VISION:

1. Write down your vision.
2. What is it you want?
3. What time frame are you wanting to achieve it?
4. Make a Vision Board (make it yours, Claim it)

5. You can write down your visions and things you want to do, or cut out pictures.
6. Put it in a place where you can see it.
7. See it every day.
8. Write down your statements of positivity, your mantra.
9. Meditate on each item you have on your board.
10. Journal about your experience afterwards (stream of conscious).

Making the Vision Board, journaling, and meditating will support you in getting the momentum going, moving in the direction of your dreams.

Acting as if your goal has already occurred, that what you want is already waiting for you.

If what you are reaching for seems out of reach and another way to achieve your goal pops up, is it a wrong choice? No, it's not a wrong choice, it is just approaching it from a different perspective.

I often hear people say on Monday or Tuesday," I can't wait till Friday, because it will be the weekend." The assumption is, then they will be happy.

I said to someone "Why can't you be that happy on a Monday or Tuesday?"

They will often say, "What do you mean?"

My reply is always, "Change your perspective. Take the same exuberance you feel about getting to the end of the week, say Friday, and instead take that same feeling, emotion, and incorporate it into Monday and the other days of the week."

I then ask if they are willing to give it a try? They would look at me first, dumb founded. It was too simple. The next day when I walked by them, I would say, "Happy Tuesday, Friday."

The best part is they always smile, and get it.

It is just changing your perspective, a small victory, piece by piece. The cost is nothing monetarily, though it may feel uncomfortable, ultimately it brings about a shift and a change in your perspective. Positive vibrations cause a ping pong effect, which then echoes to the Universe. One small victory, leads to other small victories.

I am sure you have seen someone build a snowman, or rolling a ball of snow, as it moves along it grows bigger, moving faster down the hill, picking up more snow as it moves along. It is the same in your life, moving forward, in the direction you want to go. Sure, you will pick up some twigs and dirty snow along the way, but it doesn't mean you stop at the first twig, or rock on your path. Will you hit obstacles? Of course you will, plenty of them, but it is how you act or react to each situation. There will be plenty thrown at you that will change your path, but it doesn't mean it will change your vision or your goal. But how again are you going to act or react, are you Victim or Victor to the obstacles that open new possibilities.

On my way to reaching my goals, one of the most impactful events that changed my perspective, was the passing of my oldest son Douglas, who was killed on Feb 17th, 1997.

The US Marines came to tell me and took over handling all the arrangements.

I was so numb. The pain was so deep and the emptiness so vast. I had to really look deep to the depths of my inner being to move forward after such a tragic loss. My faith in God also helped me, but the greatest help came from my son himself, who often said to me, "Mom you always see beauty in everything, even a small stone." And that became my Mantra, to assist me in moving forward.

How Choosing to see the beauty even in a small stone, is a shift in perception, like finding the extraordinary in the ordinary. Others might say making lemonade out of lemons or choosing victor over victim.

This mantra, became my new perspective, like painting on a canvas. To see a painting in a different perspective, you would turn the canvas upside down and take a step back.

WAYS TO CHANGE YOUR PERSPECTIVE:

1. Drive a different way to work or school, give it a try.
2. Smile more often.
3. Say hello to a stranger.
4. Compliment someone.
5. Take a long walk, even in the rain, (as a kid, we wouldn't hesitate to jump in a puddle)
6. Get up extra early to meditate, see the sunrise
7. Watch the sunset.

Often, we get so busy making a living that we forget to get living. Where can you turn the canvas upside down in your daily life, don't be afraid to do it.

It is sometimes the little things we do each day, or the small changes in perception that take us onward on our journeys.

It is when we get stuck, and get into a funk, that we start to lose traction. This is usually because we start with negative thoughts and words, which creates negative feelings. It's like we are trying to build a snowman by rolling the snow uphill. It feels like the circumstance owns you, which is again feeling like the victim, instead of being the victor.

A powerful tool, when you want to transition from victim to victor, is to start with small things. Such as simple changes in language. For example, you can say to yourself, today is Marvelous Monday, instead of just Monday, a Terrific Tuesday, instead of just Tuesday, a Wonderful Wednesday, a Transcendent Thursday, a Fabulous

Friday, or Super Saturday etc. It sounds so simple, but it can become contagious.

Mr. Curry's advice has taken me up and down many roads, mountains and valleys. I've had many great blessings to travel the world. I remember on a plane bound for India, looking around at all the other people in Business Class with me. Then my mind went back to High School, and how I didn't even think I would graduate, and now here I was heading alone to a country I have never been to, and getting to travel business class instead of economy. I thought about how Mr. Curry, my English teacher, whether he knew it or not, had changed my perspective and my life on so many levels.

As I headed to India, I was once again, scared and alone as I had been in high school, but I recognized India was an opportunity for something more. I could have spiraled down with negative thoughts of all the things that could go wrong, but instead I focused on a list of 100 things I wrote before I left, which were part of my vision.

I kept my thoughts and actions open to great things and great people. It changed my perspective about each country I went to and the people I met. I was traveling alone, to countries like India, the Philippines and South America, but because of my vision of the 100 things, and my ability that I learned from Mr. Curry to take a different road, I could own my fear, rather than my fear owning me, and be a victor not the victim.

We hear all the time, "life is a Journey, not a destination", that is so true! Each of us are unique and have our own journey and lessons to learn along the way, and relationships to form. We have so much to give to others, I am not talking just monetary. When you are out and about during your day, how many people do you try to talk to? How many people do you give a small compliment to? Are you going your own way, doing your own thing, not even trying to see things in a different perspective?

Many times, just a warm smile, can change not only your day, but the person who you smiled at.

We have become a society of technology, everywhere you go, people are on their cell phones. I have seen families sitting together at restaurants, instead of talking to each other, they peer at their phones every few minutes, often without looking at those that are sitting right in front of them. Let's put the phones down, and engage with those that are with us. You don't want to be a victim to your phone, you want to be a victor, and you don't want the people sitting with you to be a victim of your phone either. It changes the whole perspective, bringing back to a time of conversation. Taking time for those that we love and care about.

When was the last time you really took the time to look deep into yourself and your friends and loved ones, and asked, what is your Vision, where do you want to go, see and do?

What do you want for yourself, your family? How can you get there?

I am so very thankful for my teacher, Mr. Curry who took the time and gave a damn, about me, and opened my eyes to seeing the world in a completely different perspective. It sounds so simple, to take a different route to school or work. He was basically letting me know, don't settle, open your heart, not just your mind, be creative in life. There are many opportunities out there for you once you set your destination.

Even if the route we are taking isn't the road we set out on, we can be creative, sometimes changing our thoughts on the situation we are in and being clear with our vision. Keeping focus on our direction, and changing perspective can be as simple as taking time away from the situation. Whether it be a few minutes, hours or days. Before returning to your path continuing with fresh eyes.

Basically, taking a Step Left to gain a whole new perspective on what we are trying to work towards, change or even fix. Victim to Victor.

We have choices, and we get to choose what will serve us and support us in the best way. If a flood was coming your way, would you stay in its path or take a step left to get out of its way? The choice is yours to make!

Take a Step Left and enjoy the Journey of Life!

Casandra Carmine

***

To Contact Casandra:

Casandra Carmine

908-489-7370

Carmine.casandra@gmail.com

Touchmovenspire@gmail.com

www.Touchmoveandinspire.com

www.facebook.com/CasandraCarmine

Doug Herold

Doug has over 26 years of experience in the Food Industry, having worked in the Warehouse, Maintenance, and Operations for Sara Lee Foods, The Wornick Co. and Zwanenburg Food Group USA. After successfully incorporating the Toyota Production System, Doug was promoted to Vice President of Manufacturing at Wornick Foods. In 2016, Doug was promoted to Global Vice President of Continuous Improvement for Baxter Food Group. Throughout his career, Doug has worked to use servant leadership to drive employee engagement and continuous improvement. With a deep understanding of his field, Doug has a passion to teach the wholeness of life and leadership by "Touching People for Time and Eternity". In 2014, Doug founded Time and Eternity Inc, a personal and professional leadership development company that seeks to train people to reach their fullest potential by continuous improvement and engagement of others.

Doug and his siblings were raised by their grandparents on a farm in Grant's Lick, Kentucky. He earned a Bachelor of Divinity from the Blue Ridge Bible College and has pastored for over 20 years, starting two churches in Northern Kentucky. Doug has been married to Tammie (Sebastian) Herald for nearly 30 years, and they have three daughters.

Personal Development

By Doug Herold

Personal development starts, for most of us, with a longing. A longing inside of us to be different, a longing that tells us that there has got to be more. I want to encourage you to follow that longing. To feed it. To love it. To nurture it. To give to it. Don't ignore it. Don't assume that because others don't have it that it is wrong. One of the greatest things you will ever learn is that what you have is yours. Your gifts, your talents, and your story may not be understood by others, but they are yours. Everyone has a different story, but we all have a longing that needs to be fed.

When I turned 40, I had made it farther in my career than I ever thought I would, let alone what the rest of my world thought. Then I hit a plateau and began to feel guilty about being successful. That guilt came from the lies that I had told myself all those years, lies we all tell ourselves. We say to ourselves, "You're not worthy. You're not good enough. You can't do it." The passion that drives us to find our purpose and make ourselves better is the same passion that drives us to self-destruct if we're not careful. At that point, I decided to start investing in myself. I searched myself to discover what things in my life kept me from wanting to be all that I could be, because there was a part of me that wanted to be all that I could be, and there was a part of me that was terrified of being all that I could be. I kept thinking of how many people I would be able to help at the age of 50 if I invested in myself for those next ten years. I turned 50 on August 5, 2016, and in the past several years I've been able to help thousands of people. That emotional investment in myself has helped me to understand my past and understand that it is okay to live in the present and that it is okay to be passionate about the future. Your life may have been rough, but there are always stories of triumph and stories of defeat. Those stories are based on what we do with the opportunities we've been given and whether we chose to fight or run. As you begin to invest in yourself, that desire to run will become smaller than the willingness to fight to reach your full potential.

My journey towards personal development began over a lunch table when a friend of mine, John D'Agostino asked me one of the most profound questions that I have ever been asked. We were role-playing for my upcoming job interview, and he asked me what I was doing to develop myself. Honestly, I'd never thought about that question that way. Obviously I had done a lot to develop myself, but I never did it with a plan or a passion. I certainly never did it with the purpose of reaching my full potential. The day that John asked me that question changed my life forever. John asked it in the context of a job interview, where the emphasis is not on selling the past or the present, but rather, the future. In order to do that, we must be able to paint our future as something different from our present. People are looking for the potential that you can add to their companies, their communities, and their lives.

Our society does not pressure people to grow. So many young people are stuck in the same rut that their parents or grandparents have been stuck in, and they give up by the age of 30. They've already decided that this is all their life is ever going to be. I suppose that there's probably nothing more miserable in all the world than coming to a point in life where you think that this is all there's ever going to be, where you think that you're going to get up on Monday morning and spend all week waiting for Friday, and then you're going to do it all over again the next week. I think that's one of the saddest things that people confront, because there is more to life than a Monday through Friday job. Yes, jobs are necessary for life. But what is that job fueling? That job should be the fuel for you to do your purpose. That job should be the fuel for you to reach out and fulfill what you want to do in life. Most people, when they get somewhere between 35 and 55, hit a wall. Perhaps you've hit that wall because you're empty inside, because you've done everything that somebody else told you to do in order to be successful or happy. And for a while, you told yourself that you were happy because you were successful. But there was still that longing on the inside, the longing to reach your full potential. Personal development is critical for you, because it will affect every aspect of your life, whether as a parent, a spouse, a friend, an employee, an employer, or an entrepreneur. Mark Twain said, "The two most important days of your life are the day that you were born, and the day that you find out why." Viktor Frankl said, "Those who have a 'why' to live, can bear almost any 'how.'" That's purpose. And the way to find your purpose is through personal development. When you figure out the reason you were born, then you can begin to make a greater difference in your own life and in the lives of others.

As a leader, you must keep investing in yourself so that those you serve don't hit a glass ceiling. As a member of humanity, you must keep investing in yourself so that others can enjoy the things that come from you as you reach your potential. Life is to be lived in a way that is continually improved. I don't believe that once traditional education is done we should stop learning. When traditional education is done, we should go out into the real world and be ever learning in order to keep growing and keep doing things that are different and better. The most important thing that you can give to the world is your reaching your full potential. The second most important thing that you can give to the world is to help others reach their full potential. We are all different, yet we're all similar because we're here, and we've been given unique gifts to help each other. The only way that you're ever going to be able to help others to the maximum of your potential is if you continue to grow.

Think of life as an apple tree. That apple tree could be treated one of two ways. It could be disrespected, abused, and not appreciated. It could never be nurtured or watered or have sunlight. And then eventually it dies, and we cut it down, and we remember that apple tree fondly. We think of how nice it was when it produced apples and how beautiful it was in the springtime when it had flowers. But it's dead, so we cut it down and then burn it or use the wood for something else. That apple tree is gone forever, just like life if we don't nurture it, if we don't take care of it and invest in it, if we don't get to the point, and don't see a need to give to ourselves and then give back to others. So many lives could be great but aren't anything because people don't invest in themselves. They think that personal development is selfish, but the most selfish thing you could ever do is not reach your full potential. And the only way that you reach your full potential is by investing, by giving, and by putting back inside of you what you need in order to grow.

I grew up on a farm. I remember that every spring we would do a whole lot of work and then the next day we'd go look at the field and there would be nothing there. So what's the farmer doing? He's planting with the confidence of reaping. That's what you're doing when you invest in yourself. People today want quick results. Everybody wants something that's shallow instead of deep. You say, "I want to be. I want to be. I want to be." Yet you've never done anything in order to be. I had a friend that always said that everybody wants to start where grandpa died. But we have to start where he started and work our way to who we want to be. Quite frankly, in order to reap the way you want to reap, you must be willing to sow. You must be willing to work hard.

When John asked me that question at lunch that day, I knew I needed to begin developing myself. I started using books, audio books, and YouTube videos to learn. I can't tell you how much money I've spent on books. Jim Rohn said it best: "You're going to give somebody $30, and you get all of their life's wisdom in one little book. That's a pretty good deal." Most books aren't even $30. Most books are $15-25. For you to be able to take that $15-25 and pick the minds of great people is something special. Attending seminars also helped me invest in myself. I went to Scotland for an eight-day seminar. I went to Los Angeles for another one. I've gone all over the world to learn and grow. I wanted to grow, but the only thing that I had was the seed. And I knew from my upbringing that if I put the seed in the ground, it would do the job. If I made it, anybody can make it. But you're not going to make it by not putting in the work. So when you read this, and you ask yourself what you're doing to develop yourself, that's a critical question. That's a question that all of us should want to answer.

Today there are countless ways to grow to your full potential without spending a dime. There are amazing life coaches, seminars, and books that will help you invest in yourself. You may believe that you can't afford to invest in yourself. I believe that you can't afford not to. The greatest investment you'll ever make is in yourself growing as a person, in your field, and in your passion. When you take that apple tree of your life, and you begin to invest in it, water it, give it sunshine, it begins to grow. And as it grows, as you grow, the rest of the world gets to enjoy the flowers and the fragrance and the fruit of a life reaching its full potential.

I'm a firm believer in mentors. I'm a firm believer in finding people that are where you want to be and asking them to help you. It's amazing how many people are willing to mentor for little or no money. And even if it does cost money, why aren't we willing to pay for a life coach for ourselves? We pay for doctors. We pay for cab drivers. We pay for accountants. We pay for everything. So why wouldn't we be willing to make the investment in ourselves and pay for a mentor? If you follow the life of any successful person, you'll see that they have a coach. They have a mentor.

As you start to grow, you're going to find very quickly where your comfort zone is. It's important for you to understand that personal development will stretch you past it. And if your purpose is no bigger than your comfort zone, you'll never leave it. The only time we grow is when we get outside of our comfort zone. It's when somebody who hates to call people picks up a phone. It's when somebody who isn't comfortable talking to strangers starts opening his or her mouth. That's getting out of your comfort zone. Unless you're willing to be uncomfortable, you will not grow. One of the greatest things that you have to overcome is thinking that failure is bad. Failure is a major part of success. You will never have one without the other. Failure is an event. It's not a person or an identity. You have to be willing to fail. And the faster you fail, the sooner you will succeed. The world may mock. The world may laugh. But if you look at any successful person throughout history, they're known for their successes. They've had hundreds of failures to reach those successes. So as you go through this process, understand that failure is a huge part of the progress of your personal growth.

As you start to grow, not only will you find where your comfort zone is, but you will also find where other people's comfort zone for you is. You'll learn quickly that people have a box for you. Right now, you fit nicely inside of that box. But the moment that you start growing and get out of that box, people are going to try to put you back in it. Before you know it, you're going to be too big to go back in their box. Many people will be uncomfortable with your newfound growth. People will try to stop you. They'll try to discourage you. They won't understand why you're not doing the same things that you've always done, going to the same places that you've always gone, or hanging around the same people that you've always hung around with. It's important that you don't let that make you bitter. You don't have to justify your leaving their world. Some of those people that are uncomfortable will be people that truly love you, so they will accept the change despite the discomfort. Some may even grow with you. But a lot of people are going to be uncomfortable with the fact that you're not the way you always have been, and they're not going to be willing to accept the change in you. That's where you might have to start letting some people go. Dan Peña, one of my mentors, says, "Show me your friends, and I'll show you your future." There's a lot of truth in that. Your outlook is probably the average of the five people you spend the most time with. As you begin to develop yourself, your friends will begin to change. That's not a bad thing. It's been said that when your five closest friendships begin to change, you should make sure to replace them with people that are better. Because you're wanting to grow. You're wanting to move forward. Relationships change. Friendships change. But I believe that you don't want things to be the way that they have always been.

I often say that, when we were born, the world laughed, and we cried. I believe that we should strive to live life so that when we die, the world will cry, and we can laugh. But you only do that by hard work. Even if you are able to "make it" financially, if your purpose is big enough, you're going to continue to grow. Money doesn't change people; money simply manifests who people are. I've been asked before how much money I want to retire with, but I really believe that I'll never retire. I believe my life will change. I believe my lifestyle will change. I believe that I will move forward in different areas. I believe that I'll be in third-world countries teaching leadership and personal development. I believe that I'll be speaking all over the world, and I'll be doing things differently. I think that I owe it to this world to reach my full potential, and so do you.

People ask when personal development ends. I believe it ends in one of two ways. It ends when you reach a point in your life when your faculties are no longer able to support your continued growth, or it ends with your life. If you truly have a passion for your own personal development, you live your life continuously improving. You never stop growing because you have an ongoing desire to see those you are trying to help keep growing, and in order for that to happen, you must keep growing too. You may grow in different ways, but you keep growing. You become wiser over time, but you stay hungry. Learning and developing yourself only ends at your funeral. But until then, I believe that the most fulfilling thing that you will ever do in your life is personal development. You are worth investing in.

I ask you what John asked me, "What are you doing to develop yourself?"

***

www.timeandeternity.net

www.teleadership.us

Twitter: @TimeEternity

Gina Grahame

Gina Grahame personifies an empowering message for us all: the importance of digging deep within one's self and doing what it takes to live true to what we find. To 'live true' means challenging conventional boundaries and determining your own values and definition of success. It means risking rejection by those closest to us.

Born male, Gina became a national award winning speaker, successful actor, and model. However, our outer shell does not always reflect who we are at core. Gina spiraled into depression and attempted suicide. She awoke with a new sense of strength and a belief that she could, and would, 'be authentacious®'.

Gina transitioned to female. She created a fashion line and co-founded a mobile software company. She rebooted her life again by moving across the country to become a six-figure earning Global Sales Manager in the videogame industry.

Gina is an international award winning speaker, B2B consultant, and personal empowerment coach.

She is the founder of '25 and Rising', a diversity focused consulting business specializing in transgender and non-binary policies, and a Board Member of the Golden Gate Business Association, the nation's first and longest running LGBT Chamber of Commerce in San Francisco.

Be the Hero of Your Own Life!
Change Your Narrative and You'll Change Your Life
By Gina Grahame

Are you the Hero of your own life? If not, then who are you? Are you the Bystander? Are you the Victim? Or are you the Hero?

Mahatma Ghandi said, "A man is but the product of his thoughts. What he thinks, he becomes." I interpret this adage as, 'Change your narrative, and you'll change your life!'

We can't control the events that shape our lives, but we can control how we react to them and the role we assign ourselves in our narrative. Whether it's done consciously or unconsciously, spoken aloud or within our heads, we assign ourselves a role. And we have three choices:

We can be the Bystander, disengaged, ambivalent to the outcome as we watch the events of our lives unfold.

We can be the Victim, believing we are powerless, and choosing to let circumstances and the actions of others determine our fate.

We can be the Hero, actively pushing our lives forward toward goals, dreams, and personal happiness, while providing an example and inspiration to others.

Being the Hero of your own life is at the core of my 'be authentacious®' philosophy. To 'be authentacious®' is to be your best unique self and to empower others to do the same. It's being bold, proactive, and empathic to the those around you that differentiates what it is to be authentic from what it is to be authentacious®.

Real Heroes aren't superhuman or saints. They don't possess mythological powers or go through life without fear or regret. They're real people like you and me; the people you see every day on your way to work, in the grocery store, or waiting for the next bus. They are individuals who understand the difference between getting beaten and being beaten. They get knocked down, often in unimaginable ways, and then find the courage and strength to get up one more time. Rocky Balboa isn't an iconic character for stepping into in the boxing ring with the World Champion; he's iconic because he rose to his feet even when his mentor was telling him to stay down.

Maya Angelou's story did not end with her being raped and abused at age eight, or working in the sex industry while a teenager and single mother. Maya channeled and redirected those experiences to become a civil rights activist, singer, actor, and one of the 20th Century's most prolific authors, winning the Pulitzer Prize and the Presidential Medal of Freedom among countless other awards.

Malala Yousafzai was 14 years old when she boarded a school bus in her home village in Pakistan. A Taliban gunman boarded, asked for her by name, put a pistol to her head and fired three shots. Her crime was speaking out on the rights of girls to go to school. During her extensive recuperation, Malala continued to speak out. In 2013, at just 17 years old, she became the youngest recipient of Nobel Peace Prize. Malala remains a leading voice for equal rights for women and girls worldwide, and is still considered to be a target for the Taliban.

If you're thinking these examples are of extraordinary people living through extraordinary circumstances, let me share a personal story. This may shock and upset you. I share it not to be controversial, but because after every seminar I have given, at least one woman in attendance has approached me privately to share a similar personal story with me.

I'm continually astonished by how common this experience is among women. That sense of shame and the belief the violent incident was somehow their fault, is something I know well and am determined to do my part to stop. This is the reason that I share my story with you.

See if you can tell which role I cast for myself.

I attended a work conference in Vancouver in 2010. It was late Spring; warm enough to wear a t-shirt during the day, yet you could still see snow atop the mountains that line Cole Harbor. While walking with a colleague toward the convention center, a guy I'd never met before stopped me and asked if I'd go out with him. I declined.

He must have read the event badge around my neck because he showed up at the conference the next day and found me. He began by apologizing for coming on so strongly and then asked me to join him for a drink. He was well dressed, charming, and classically tall, dark and handsome, so I agreed.

Later that evening we had a drink and conversation. As dusk approached, we walked the two blocks to the waterfront to continue our conversation and watch the sunset.

Half-way down the street, we were walking under the construction lattice work of a building when he suddenly shoved me into a small alleyway. He pinned me to the wall, his forearm pressing into my throat so tightly that I could barely breath. He sexually assaulted me. When he finally backed off me, he had the nerve to think our evening would continue. When he was a step in front of me and began to turn left, I ran to right until I was sure he wasn't following.

I didn't go the police. I was only in the country for one more day and did not want to bring any negative attention to the conference or to myself.

What voice do you hear in this story, the Hero? The Bystander? The Victim? If you're not sure, let me tell you the story from a slightly different perspective.

My work sent me to Vancouver in 2010. It was a beautiful, late Spring day; the flowers were blooming and you could still see snow capping the mountains around Cole Harbor.

My colleague asked me to join her at a business meeting. While walking to the restaurant, a guy stopped me on the street and asked me out. I was so shocked at his boldness, I reflexively said no.

He must have followed us because half-way through the dinner meeting he showed up at our table, sat down next to me, and asked me out again. I was so embarrassed at how this must have made me look in the eyes of the client and my colleague.

He must have seen the event badge around my neck because he showed up at the conference the next day. He apologized for the previous meeting interruption, was charming, and looked like the poster boy for 'tall, dark, and handsome.' I admit that I kind of liked his persistence so I said 'yes' to the offer of a drink.

The restaurant we met in was very populated, so I felt very comfortable. He spoke openly about himself, his travels, and why he liked being a boxer and mixed martial arts fighter. He asked to continue our discussion along the waterfront as the sun was beginning to set.

He held my hand as we walked under the construction lattice work of a nearby building. Suddenly, he shoved me into a small alleyway and pinned me against the wall. His left forearm was so tight against my throat that I could barely breathe, much less scream. He shoved his right hand into my pants. I felt powerless. I asked him to stop, but he didn't. I prayed someone would see what he was doing and say or do something, anything, to make him stop. But no one did.

I knew I was no match him for him physically. I can still see the smirk on his face as he did whatever he wanted to do. He stopped; but only long enough to move his hand from the front of my pants to the back. When he finally backed off me, he motioned for us to continue our walk.

He was in front of me as we stepped back onto the street. I waited until he turned left and then I turned right and ran, not stopping until I was sure he wasn't following me. I went back to my room, double locked the door, and fell onto the bed, crying. I was so ashamed that I'd let this happen to when I should have known better.

I didn't go the police because I didn't want to bring any negative attention to the conference or myself for fear of being fired. When I confided in a friend the next day, she shared a personal story of abuse from her past. While I found comfort in not being alone, hearing her story shocked and made me even despondent.

Who am I this version? Can you see you a difference in the words I use? Let me tell you the story once more…

I had the opportunity to go to Vancouver in late Spring, 2010. I'd always wanted to go and since I had recently obtained a promotion and would be attending a conference, I'd get to see it on someone else's dime – score!

The weather was gorgeous. The flowers were all in bloom and you could still see snow atop the mountains that line the north end of Cole Harbor. I was walking along the street with a colleague when a guy stopped me and asked me out. I knew better than to agree to a drink with some random stranger and continued on our way.

The next day at the conference I arrived at the Information Center to find the guy from the day before. He apologized for being so forward and then asked me to join him for one drink that evening. He was good looking, tall, very physically fit, and with enough charm to have me saying 'ok.'

Later that evening we met in a very public restaurant, away from my hotel. After a while, I agreed to walk with him along the waterfront to watch the sunset. We were passing an alley way when I suddenly found myself shoved against a brick wall. His left forearm was so tight against my throat that I could hardly breathe, much less scream. With his right hand, he began to sexually assault me. I had learned over our drink that he was professional fighter and, realizing I was not a physical threat to this man, I chose to lose all emotion drain from my face and simply stare into his eyes, just inches from my own. My lack of resistance surprised and eased him back somewhat.

"Are you through?" I asked. He continued. Again, my lack of response made him pause. "Are you through now? Then get your hand out of my pants." He backed off of me. He motioned toward the street and for me to walk ahead of him. "After you" I said. When we reached the street, he turned to the left and I immediately ran to the right, yelling at an unseen, make-believe friend, and got away.

After I created some distance from the event and talked it through with a therapist, I realized I had gotten away from a professional fighter who was bigger, and stronger than I; and I had done so without getting raped, beaten, or killed in the process.

Who am I this version? Which version of this story do you think I tell and why?

Yes, this is the version I tell myself and others when recounting the incident. Why? Because I am the Hero.

It's important to note that I did not tell myself the Hero version immediately. Far from it. Initially, I blamed myself for everything; for getting into the situation in the first place, for 'not being smarter', and for buying into the storybook idea of the tall, dark & handsome stranger and a foreign sunset.

Days went by before I could see how I was casting myself as the victim. And worse yet, by doing so, I had absolved him of any responsibility as the attacker. I began to realize I could acknowledge I had been victimized without having to cast myself as the victim.

In each version, I find myself in a position I had no intention of being in and would have done anything to avoid. But it's only in the third version where the 'Third Act' of my personal Hero's Journey takes place.

The Third Act began with the most crucial step: forgiving myself. Forgiving myself was like removing a crushing weight from my shoulders. Forgiving myself allowed me to observe how changing the words I used to describe the incident elicited very different emotions within me and impacted my self-confidence and self-image. Forgiving myself also removed the clock from time needed to heal. I was free to experience setbacks, knowing they were only temporary and that I was on the right path.

Because of the Third Act, I'm not just the Hero at the end of the story; the use of action words when retelling reaffirms my position as the Hero throughout.

The Hero's Journey is never easy. I am in no way minimizing the real and deep effects of Post-Traumatic Stress Disorder (PTSD). Nor would I offer any advice to those who are suffering with it other than encourage them that they seek direct, professional assistance.

The Bystander

The Bystander is a role which allows us to avoid being the Victim, but also prevents us from seeing ourselves as the Hero. The Bystander is unemotional, neither positive nor negative, choosing to simply be a spectator. Bystanders don't assign blame, responsibility, or have a desired outcome. Much like witnesses on TV police dramas when characters are asked for 'just the facts, ma'am. Just the facts,' the Bystander's narrative is dry, terse, and removed.

The narrative of the Bystander contains words of non-commitment and distance/separation. Key words used by the bystander are third-person pronouns (he/she, them, it), Impersonal language ('this guy/woman/person').

The Victim

The Victim can take many forms, from the helpless recipient of activity to blaming others to avoid personal responsibility. The victim can believe, consciously or subconsciously, that they are somehow unworthy of being the Hero. Therefore, they are somehow deserving of the actions others perpetrate against them. Even if they don't believe themselves to be a true victim, they may use the words of the Victim to elicit sympathy or martyr themselves.

The narrative of the Victim contains words of exploitation and loss/failure/injury. The Key words used by the victim are Always, Never, They, Why, Fault

The Hero

The Hero isn't about being Superman or Wonder Woman. It's not about being impervious to pain, disappointment or setbacks; it's about understanding and accepting that those emotions will emerge, yet choosing to move forward with what you know is right and just. It's about taking an active role in your daily life and believing you can, and do, make a difference in the lives of those around you.

The narrative of the Hero contains words of personal action and achievement.

Key words used by the Hero are: I, Can, Am, Will, Choose, Choice

We chose the lens through which we view our life events and once time allows us to choose that lens with more wisdom. Look at the three versions of my story above and notice again how the words I use define my role: first as the Bystander, then the Victim, and lastly as the Hero.

You may be thinking, 'I'm glad you were able to be the Hero in your story. But I've never been through anything like that. So how does this help me?'

The need and opportunity to act, to be the Hero of your own story, is everywhere!

One of my clients was woman named Donna. Donna was in her late 50's and stressed because her job in local government was ending after nearly twenty years and she was unable to find a new job.

"I'm a secretary," she replied to my initial query. I began my response by letting her know that 'secretary' was an outdated term best left to 'Mad Men' reruns. As I inquired deeper into her duties and responsibilities, her answers revealed a very different truth. She maintained the schedule of her boss, a senior official, worked on budgets, purchasing, staff procedures and policies. And at home, Donna helped her husband start a business by researching, purchasing, and helping to run the machinery, boxing and shipping orders, doing the bookkeeping, and handling the social media advertising.

As you can see, Donna is anything but just 'a secretary.' She's a multi-faceted bad-ass entrepreneur who gets things done! Once she changed the narrative of her story to see herself as a person of action, the Hero, she began applying for positions she never would have considered herself qualified for before. Soon, she accepted the offer of her choosing instead of feeling trapped into accepting the first offer to come along.

My challenge to you:

Think of an incident within your own life that had real impact and that you revisit at times in your mind. This can be a divorce, a sudden loss of your job, a personal tragedy from your childhood.

Get together with a trusted loved one. In person is best, though over-the-phone will do. If you feel the story is too personal to share, then use the recorder function on your mobile phone in private.

Set a timer for three minutes

Tell your story

At the end of the three minutes, have your loved one tell if you were the Hero, the Victim, or the Bystander by the words you used in your story.

Insights into Self-Empowerment

If you are satisfied with what you hear, then great! If not, then then tell your story again while choosing more empowering words and statements.

Bonus points by repeating the exercise with your loved on telling a story to you!

Remember, it's not the events that shape our fates, it's the role we play within events. You can be the Hero. Change your narrative and you'll change your life!

***

To contact Gina:

Email: gina@ginagrahame.com

Website: www.BeAuthentacious.com

Facebook: www.facebook.com/BeAuthentacious

Instagram: www.instagram.com/BeAuthentacious

Twitter: www.twitter.com/GinaGrahame

#BeAuthentacious

LinkedIn: https://www.linkedin.com/in/GinaGrahame

Shop 'be authentacious':
https://squareup.com/store/BeAuthentacious

Margo Massard

I experience so much joy helping people be who they truly be. My journey is the blueprint; if I can do it, anyone can! I know everything I've created in my life, has been not only a gift but exactly that, MY creation. That being said, I am called now to go within, deepen my knowledge of my authentic self, seek information, illumination as to how best to express my purpose on this planet. And most importantly, to discover the wellspring of my divine self and, much like the phoenix, arise from the ashes of the deconstruction of ego, as pure love energy.

Being Me

By Margo Massard

The invitation to contribute to this publication came in direct response to my request of the Universe to show me my next step in expressing my purpose, how I could best contribute to the wellbeing of our planet and its inhabitants. This is the most recent manifestation I've created since I began this portion of my journey of spiritual transformation over a year and a half ago.

The synchronicity and the ease with which everything has fallen into place never ceases to delight me to my very core. When I look back at the changes I've affected in my life over the past ten years, I can only be thankful I finally chose to listen to that all too often disregarded inner voice. I had developed sudden onset double vision, hadn't enjoyed a good nights' sleep in months, and barely earned enough money to support myself and my then 15 year-old special-needs daughter. Sounds like so many other peoples' stories, doesn't it?

I acknowledge and own that I created all of it and remain, to this day, grateful for every moment; indeed, I consider that period a gift beyond price, for those events opened the door to learning a whole new way of functioning on this planet. It did not, let me assure you, happen overnight. Indeed, as stubborn and stuck in old programming and behaviors as any person could be, I took another two years before landing in the program that would start me on my path to rediscovering my true nature and another four years to take the quantum leap into truly acknowledging, accepting and embracing the gift I be to the Universe.

Even now I have the tendency, the knee-jerk reaction, to self-efface, to pretend I'm less than the awesome being I truly be. That I can override the trigger reactions I attribute to years of practice using, on a daily basis, the tools I've accumulated; cultivating awareness through meditation, monitoring my thoughts, and last, but certainly not least, intensive body work, the benefits of which include releasing, down to the cellular level, the judgments (by self and others), beliefs, programming anchored in my body by the density of this reality and the intensity of my then reality. This last component, I have to say, has offered me more freedom than I can express. My body, after all it's been subjected to for over 6 decades, never ceases to amaze me with its ability to recreate itself; from sexual abuse to falling down mountains to being hit by cars, to healing others by taking on their stuff (resulting in numerous surgeries), to regenerate itself, to provide me with information (now that I ask!), to contribute to the synergetic beingness of ME; all this in exchange for heartfelt, sincere expressions of acknowledgement, honor, gratitude and certainly, love.

Which brings me to the fulcrum around which all that I be, do and have, revolves – Love: divine, unconditional, transformational, transcendent... the list could go on and on. When I began designing my website almost three years ago, I had no notion how that would look or where it would lead. Out of that organic process a theme emerged. Heart-centered healing, heartfelt emotion, a collage of heart images; clearly, I needed this. As I expanded into the energy of heart, of divine love, I was led, slowly, inexorably, down a path which opened up connection to Divine Source, the knowledge of my own divinity, seeing the Christ as the loving light he embodies. That is my quest - to vibrate at that level of love and light, seeing perfection in every moment, in everything.

All I have created since then has been to that end; to embody the divine love we all be, to raise the vibration of this planet through focused thought energy strengthened through vibrational alignment with other compatible energies. And of course, to create in three dimensional reality, what will assist in bringing about the desired outcome of raising the vibration of our planet. Again, I have no idea what that looks like; only what it feels like. I know I will be led to the necessary people, places and means necessary to create and generate whatever is required.

I know now every event that has occurred in this lifetime (indeed, any lifetime) I created for the evolution of my soul. I embrace this. I embrace those I once termed predators and thank them for being willing to play the "bad" guy for me to work through my lessons. I am grateful. I also know I chose a female body and set up the sexual molestations, rape, and abuse because I had molested, raped and abused many over the course of my numerous incarnations. We have all been and done everything. To ourselves and to others. I am at peace with that knowledge; it has helped liberate me from many of the denser, earthbound vibrations we are all familiar with - judgment, resentment, guilt, shame, and blame. It has also gifted me the (learned) ability to stand back (most of the time) and allow others the space to create what they need to fulfil their purposes on this planet.

Every experience we create is a gift to our souls, and by extension, to all of us, isn't it? Once we step out of judgment of the good, bad, right, or wrong of anything and own that we created it all, we are then free to create what we truly desire, whatever that may be. Functioning from the lightness and love of source opens a whole new way of being on this planet. Esoteric terms like peace, goodwill, happiness, thriving, sharing, global wellbeing, and flourishing become realities rooted in the psyche, grounded into the earth, elevated by the Universe, enveloping the planet, nurturing and nourishing our souls and bodies.

For all it takes is sustained focus, belief and intention to bring to fruition the desired outcome.

One must believe in the possibilities that exist in every moment, the intensity of intention to create what you wish for, the focus to hold a space, with no attachment to the desired outcome. How easy can it be?

Know too, that we do this every day, several times a day, thinking nothing of it. How aware are you of your creative and generative powers? How often do you acknowledge what you create? As creative beings, we do this countless times every day. Regardless of how or whether we judge the outcome, all follows the same process. How many times have you driven into a crowded parking lot and thought, "I need a space close to the entrance" and voila, it appears, or the converse, you think, "I'll never find a space close to the entrance" and, voila, you don't. And, of course, there's always default programming to kick in should we not bother to ask!

Imagining the outcome produces, most times, that outcome. I know, too, that, as creative as we humans are, there are those of you who can cite incident after incident where the opposite is true. Which only proves the point, doesn't it? As self-determining, creative entities we easily bend reality to match our beliefs. So, for a different outcome, change your thought, change your belief. If you want to know if your life is working, look around you. What's in front of your face will tell you the truth about your life. Before you go into denial, judgment, or defense, all of which contract energetically, pause, breathe into all of that and relax. Happily, for all of us, there exists a remedy; infinite possibility. If that doesn't serve to relieve the visceral reactions mentioned above, keep breathing until some sense of equilibrium emerges from the senseless terror incited by observing what you've made real; never mind how it all came to pass. One of the advantages of having a body on this planet, aside from love of the physical beauty of earth, nature and our ability to experience that on a sentient level, is grounded in the power of choice. After introduction to the concept (never mind the exercise) of choice when I was in my 40's (yes, I'm a quick learner!), I was introduced, years later, to the power of choosing in 10 second increments. This tool opened a portal so expansive, so life-enhancing, it took years to fully incorporate into my spiritual toolbox and to this day, I often forget to use it.

I can only say for those of you whose realities, like mine, were so small and constricted, defined by others' wants and needs, the blinding realization of choice, of possessing the ability to change what feels unchangeable, represents true freedom. Imagine the rolling vistas, the panoramic landscapes, the broadened scope of vision that comes with the freedom of choosing from the field of infinite possibilities. Perhaps it feels too expansive? Choose to narrow your vision until you feel comfortable; choosing in 10 second increments, you can always grow into a more expanded version. Perhaps you fear judgment from those invested in maintaining the status quo? Choose to expand your allowance for their point of view by loving them more. Perhaps you fear making the wrong choice? Exercise the awareness you can always choose, again and again and again. To shift out of the belief in your own powerlessness into the power of choice involves honoring your own path (while allowing others theirs) even if you may not know what that path actually looks like; reach deep within yourself to trust in the Universe to aid, assist, guide and support you.

Stepping out of the contracted energy of judgment allows me to expand my awareness; how many times have you entered a room full of people and stopped dead in the doorway? Do you have the awareness you are taking the energetic pulse of the room? How you proceed from there rests on your perception of how your vibration matches up with the energy in the room. Do you align with whatever energy prevails? Do you resist? Or are you able to set and hold your own vibration? Or do you turn and hightail it out of there? Look at all the choices available just in that split second of assessment.

How much easier and more fun to note the energy of any given situation, expand into allowance (bypassing judgment) and observe, from that expanded state of awareness, whether you are vibrationally aligned, or holding your own vibration despite others'? Of course, there's always the possibility you'll be triggered, and then what? Fall into judgment of self and contract to match the prevailing vibration? Don't think I haven't. The American election this year was a great example of thousands of people matching and reacting to vibrations. I chose to match the vibration of fear, loss and denial, engaging in Facebook recriminations, sarcastic postings eliciting hostile responses before I reached my saturation point and literally shut down my computer disengaging to regain vibrational equilibrium. Even now writing about it my body remembers the sensations evoked! I take a moment, breathe in, and expand, consciously choosing to release the physical reminders of that experience. At the same time, I refocus my thoughts on something that brings me pleasure; gratitude or forgiveness always works for me as does cleansing with Ho'Oponono – for the election, all of the above!

Once you've chosen to practice the art of not judging (self or others), and felt the lightness that comes from stepping outside the heaviness of that contracted energy, life becomes more fun. While others expend energy trying to figure out this and that, judging good and bad, right and wrong, I focus my energy on connecting with source, projecting loving thought energy outward, communing with my body, nourishing Mother Earth. I ask you, of the choice between the two scenarios, which feels light for you? What resonates more at a deeper soul level?

I began my journey on this path, not as a spiritual quest, but more along the lines of, I have got to do something different or I'll die. I chose life, I chose to honor what I knew deep within; I took this body in this family in this time for a reason. I'd cheated death a number of times – all very interesting stories – knowing, under all the layers of others' energies, lay inviolate, the essence of ME.

At the beginning of my journey, however, emergency measures required triage of the soul. Among many other processes, this involved separating from other peoples' energies – a long, arduous process as I had absolutely no idea where, in all the muck, resided the tiny, flickering light I recognized on a primal level as ME! As layer after layer was peeled back, layered on again, peeled back and released (ad nauseum!), I began to see, to feel, to sense, a fluttering, a pulsing, of what I could only assume was me, a sentient being, a divine spark with my own history, my own information acquired over countless lifetimes.

I cannot articulate adequately the feelings as I dug through the detritus to unearth my unique vibrational signature, commonly known as my soul; so foreign to me, it took years until I could distinguish my vibration from other energies. As I progressed in my personal growth, moving from survival into awareness and increasing consciousness, my concept of separation shifted from rigid attention to keeping my space clear of other entities, with and without bodies, erecting protections, elaborate rituals and processes designed to keep everything outside MY SPACE, to realizing how limiting that felt. I've found protection necessarily precludes expansion; following the energy, although I didn't recognize it as such then, paved the way from functioning at survival level, what I see now as a contractive energy, to opening to perceiving, knowing, being and receiving all that the Universe has to offer. Not that this happened instantaneously but, once introduced to the concept of infinite possibilities, my soul quickened, remembering the inherent promise therein. Moving from the emphasis on separation as the governing principle into the knowing that we are all connected, we are all one, and learning new tools to facilitate the practical application of expansiveness, proved to be easy. It felt natural to me, I felt lighter expanding out to the edges of the Universe as opposed to pulling my energy in, effectively limiting my world to a five-foot diameter. And yet, out of the collective consciousness emerges individual entities; how does one reconcile the dichotomy between the all and the one?

I have learned as I move forward in my quest for knowledge of self, we each have our unique vibrational signature that distinguishes us from the whole. I have also discovered that acknowledging and fostering the connection to divine source necessarily fosters connection to the collective consciousness. Sitting in the energy of connection, emanating gratitude, love, appreciation of the ALL for all, I embrace easy, simple and fun. I think easy, simple and fun, and so it is.

The search for my truth propels me further within. I've noticed during this process certain interesting, although not surprising, awarenesses bubbling to the surface. Practicing positive self-affirmations such as telling myself "I love you" has become easier over the last couple of years. I see now that I say that to divergent, disconnected parts of me, never the whole, integrated entity that includes body, mind, spirit, conscious, unconscious, ego. This awareness invites a number of interesting sensations, observations and perceptions. Seeing all the disembodied, disassociated, severed remains formed from every experience I ever created, judged as wanting and threw to the wayside provides me the opportunity to move through loving, forgiving, thanking, into wholeness. The tendency to use intellect to disseminate experience (historically one of my favorite pastimes), has contributed, beyond the initial visceral trigger of protection from perceived threat, to nothing but accumulation of the detritus of all the parts of me I've rejected.

Choosing to be in allowance of the healing power of divine love moves me beyond limitation, enabling me to attune to this new vibration (of wholeness) rather than the dis-integrated entity. Acknowledging love heals all and allowing that energy to permeate from the inside out, I invite *me* back to myself, expanding, amplifying the love I now extend to the whole on every level, every plane of existence, every lifetime, and all cellular memory radiating out to the ALL.

Playing with the energy of wholeness, looking at me in a new way, the universe gifts me with my next vibrational step - Synergetic Being, inviting me to step into the energy of synergy. What does it mean? The dictionary definition is the interaction of elements (parts) that when combined produces a total effect that is greater than the sum of the individual elements, contributions, etc.

How does it feel? Expansive. Does it resonate deep within me? Absolutely. As I move toward wholeness, allowing all to just be rather than micro managing the bits and parts, I find myself settling into an ease only glimpsed before. How much time do we, as humans, spend hyper-focusing on some *thing* that has engaged our attention? We descend into the abyss of trying to figure it out so we can either heal it, make it go away, or just push it into the recesses of the shadow world. As I play with this energy of wholeness, acknowledging the state of synergetic beingness, my body responds more quickly, my mind releases attachment more easily, and spirit soars. All parts support, aid, and assist for the benefit of the entire organism – ME!

What I know to be true: As I move along my path to spiritual transformation I know what I currently believe to be true will shift, change and evolve at the rate I choose, in the way I allow, for this is my story.

As Above, So Below. As Within, So Without

***

To contact Margo

Margo@FlourishandThrive.us

www.FlourishandThrive.us

Robin Rose

For more than three decades, Robin Rose has explored the frontiers of leadership and neuroscience. As a keynote speaker and corporate trainer, she has an unconditional regard for human beings at work and the stress they can encounter. With a Master's degree in Counseling Psychology, Robin teaches a rare and scientific approach that allows individuals and companies to give their best while they feel their best.

Her latest book, *Shifting Gears: A Brain Based Approach to Engaging Your Best Self,* has been field tested on over 100,000 people and is packed with tools for clear thinking, improved relationships, and renewed enthusiasm for life. Robin has trained thousands of professionals who wanted to learn how their brain works, so they could think, act, and communicate at their highest proficiency.

Robin lives on a small farm in rural Oregon.

A Scientific Approach to Healthy Self-Talk
By Robin Rose

For just a few moments, think about the last stressful thing that happened to you. Notice how it feels in your body, mind, and spirit. Did your stomach tighten? Did your breathing get shallow? Is that wrinkle between your eyebrows starting to show? Are you fixated on who did you wrong and how you'd like them to pay?

There's a purpose to what you just did. Exploring the spectrum of your feelings is a starting point for discovering how unhelpful thoughts get diffused and healthy ones can return. Creating supportive self-talk requires you to identify both the hidden and obvious forces that shape your psyche. This will help you determine which are destructive versus which are kind and truthful. In this chapter, we'll use neuroscience to advance this crucial conversation.

When you categorize a thought as "positive" or "negative," you create an environment of judgement and a place of duality that lives inside of you. This makes you view yourself and others in extremes. Everything becomes either "good" or "bad," "right" or "wrong." Truth is, nothing is black or white. There are shades of grey in all of us. People also have different opinions of what's considered positive and negative. For some, having a friend vent their frustrations is healing and bonding. For others, it's considered an energy drain. The bottom line is, you are given a variety of emotions in order to experience and express them. It's your job to know which are healthy for you at a given time.

Maybe you've tried self-esteem books or positivity mantras, and you've become a believer in making people feel good. Your efforts are wise, and for many of you, there's a silent shame occurring because you haven't been able to banish your sabotaging beliefs completely. You've tried meditation and yoga, and you've even removed pessimistic people from your life. Still, the demons linger in the corners of your mind. You eventually start to wonder if there's something wrong with you. How do others remain so optimistic? Here's a little dose of reality:

Even the healthiest people have unhealthy thoughts.

When you understand why it can take effort to find your happy place, it arms you with information that 99% of the population doesn't have. It's like being handed a map to decode human psychology and find the island of peace. Are you ready to finally make this happen for yourself? Great! Let's get going!

DISCOVERY #1: What happens in your first three years of life lasts forever.

Who raised you from birth to age three? Do you remember how this person, usually Mom or Dad, responded when they were under duress? Did they shut down, scream, run away, or hide? Your caretakers likely reacted in a detrimental way at times. This didn't go unnoticed by you as a newborn and toddler. Their reactions were wired into your brain, causing you to respond the same when it happens to you. Have you ever seen a grown adult throw a tantrum? It takes many generations (some would say twenty) to change these knee-jerk reactions, unless you are committed to re-writing your brain through education and repetition therapy.

It's enlightening to explore your family's beliefs and the inherent views of those in your community. Were you raised to believe that money is the root of all evil and that people of a certain color, gender, age, or ethnicity were somehow less-than or even dangerous? Did your parents think doctors are a joke and are meant to be avoided? Did your family believe people couldn't be trusted in business or that traveling out of the country was unsafe?

These beliefs were embedded into your psyche. Until you recognize their occupancy and can see how they are affecting your decisions, they will run your life forever. Here's the good news—there's a way to grow up and become your own person!

DISCOVERY #1: You are *not* responsible for your first thought, but you *can* choose your second thought and the ones that follow.

One more time, read that last sentence. It's imperative that you allow this potentially "negative" first thought to exist, knowing it isn't who you are. It's part of your programming. Flick it away like an inconsequential piece of lint on your sweater! What is worthy of your attention are the second, third, and fourth thoughts. That's where you have control, and it's where intuition and your higher self can be accessed. This is also how discernment is gained.

If you feel like "negativity" won't stop entering your mind, take away its power. It's often said that "isms" like racism or sexism have survived in society because they've been passed down generationally. You might have a racist reaction to a person. That is your past talking. Call on your current self and invite your grown-up thoughts to emerge before acting, speaking, or judging anyone, including yourself.

DISCOVERY #2: Evidence suggests that you can have up to 60,000 self-talk moments a day and each thought has an immediate impact on your psychology.

Now remember, your brain cannot tell the difference between a real and a vividly imagined event. This is why people have panic attacks when they aren't in real harm or why others think they're overweight when they actually look fabulous and fit. A fear-based thought will signal your brain that danger exists. That is why positive affirmations have been helpful. They stop the brain from traveling into unhappy territory.

An effective way to discover the thoughts that linger in your head is to write in a journal. Allow your words to spill out on the page without censorship. Over time and upon review, you will see patterns and phrases that arise. Most of us have no idea how many unpleasant thoughts we have per day. When you see it on paper, there can be no denial. This discovery can change your life radically!

DISCOVERY #3: There are two major areas of the brain that get triggered—survival brain and thinking brain. One facilitates creativity, collaboration, and empathy. The other is only needed in emergency situations.

When you're challenged and you say to yourself, "It's okay. I can handle this," your brain perceives competence. Safety and blood flow reach your "thinking" brain. However, when you say, "Oh no, this is awful," your brain perceives threat and sends signals of panic. This is referred to as "fight, flight, or freeze." When this survival reaction occurs, the thinking brain is disengaged, and only one of them can function at a time. The survival brain cannot generate innovative solutions. That's not its job. But if you need to run from a bear or pick up an impossibly heavy object, survival brain could literally save your life.

When I work with CEOs and corporate executives, my job is to get them to stop when the pressure to meet goals is affecting their decisions. They often don't realize when their survival brain is active. Adrenaline pushes them to get more done, but it numbs their true emotions and removes them from using their "thinking" brain. This causes them to ignore what's critically important around them because their immediate need is for safety or protection.

Ever wonder why New Year's goals are rarely achieved? We tend to approach them out of disgust, rather than inspiration. And by February, we are ashamed that we didn't keep it going. Survival brain will cause you to say, "Just give up! This isn't worth it." But when you keep your thoughts optimistic and visualize success, the thinking brain finds a way to be triumphant.

DISCOVERY #4: Research indicates that up to 98% of some people's thoughts are focused on what they don't like and don't want.

After eight months of age, our brains have a negativity bias. For instance, if you're walking down a path and the left side is a steep drop-off and the right side is a field of flowers, you're going to pay attention to the cliff because your brain is wired for safety.

This is why it's natural to fixate on what goes wrong or what is fearful in your life. Being human means encountering legitimate pain. At times, it's healthy to express anger, sadness, denial, or despair. We come out of defense mode (survival brain) when we can say what's true. It takes energy to stay in denial and the body is strengthened by telling the truth. This allows your insides to match your outside. However, if you go on complaining and harboring resentment, it's no longer a "healthy vent." You're keeping yourself in survival brain.

Some people need to complain for a moment in order to see the good. When they notice what they don't like and can name it, it gives their brain a message on what improvements are desired. This helps them get out of the endless complain cycle. Personally, if I notice I am complaining or upset about something for the third time, it's time for me to take productive action.

Would you like to get into your thinking brain more quickly? Thinking brain gives you access to compassion, creativity, problem-solving, and intuition. If you find yourself feeling doubtful or stuck, try this powerful self-talk statement to turn things around, "I love and accept myself exactly as I am right now." It cuts to the core of personal distress and clicks on your thinking brain.

Here's a list for "go-to phrases" when you're feeling down or in crisis:

• It's okay.	• I can find the humor.	• We'll see our way through this.
• I can deal with this.	• I can feel myself calming down.	• What do I want to model to my kids right now?
• I will figure it out.	• I can hear myself think.	
• Yes, it's uncomfortable.	• I am strong.	• I can be patient in this moment.
• I can manage.	• I can deal with this.	• It's a good time to count to 10 or 100.
• I can choose what to focus on.	• I'm in control of myself.	
• I can be my best, even now.	• I'm bigger than this.	• I need a time out.
• Something good can come of this.	• I trust myself.	• I'm taking a walk.
• I have faith this will work out.	• I can choose.	• I'm letting this go.
• What am I/we learning?	• I can be generous right now.	• This too shall pass.
• I have the ability to handle this.	• I hear my voice coming down.	• I am going to focus on my breath for a while.
	• I can steady myself. This is workable.	• I trust my feelings.

DISCOVERY #5: Your brain does not process negatives. Instead, it produces an image or feeling about what you tell it to avoid, which actually increases what you don't want.

Unhelpful phrasing is so ingrained in our culture that we often don't realize its effects. When I say, "Don't think about standing up," I bet you thought about standing up. Why does this happen? Once again, it has to do with brain wiring. When you use negative phrasing, it inadvertently tells your brain to focus on what you're trying to avoid, even though your intention is quite the opposite.

Here are a few well-intended messages. Can you feel the energizing effects when you make the switch?

Don't worry. = It'll work out.

Don't mention it. = You're welcome.

I wouldn't leave you high and dry. = I am here for you.

No objections = Works for me.

No worries = It's okay.

When you ask for what you want, rather than what you don't want, it invites your thinking brain to take affirmative action. For example, "I'm not going to yell at Billy," could be rephrased with, "I'll stay calm when I talk with Billy." When an upset occurs at home, try using solution focused language to help your family stay resilient. Remember, your internal dialogue replicates what your parents said while they were under stress. You can change the model for your children.

DISCOVERY #6: You have eight seconds until your survival brain chemicals fully kick into gear. This gives you time to relax, find awareness, and change the direction your mind.

If you think about it, eight seconds is a long time. Still, you might be so overcome that you cannot stop those expressions from surfacing. That's why a slow deep breath in the midst of chaos can prevent emotions from exploding. Here's an example:

Sally and Joe planned to take the kids to the zoo. As they are preparing to leave, Sally tells Joe that she's invited her mom to come along. Joe thinks, "Oh no! Jane is always late. If we wait for her to show up, the whole day will be ruined." Joe feels his heart racing, and he starts to protest, but he stops. Breathing becomes his priority and tells himself, "I know Sally wants to include her mom, and Jane is pretty fun once she arrives. What can I do here?" He gives himself a minute to motivate his thinking brain. Then, he says, "Sally, I would like to take our time at the zoo and relax before tonight's barbeque. Could we ask your mom to get here early? Or maybe we can pick her up on the way? What do you think?"

Problem was solved, and it was drama-free. Smart move, Joe!

DISCOVERY #7: Moods are contagious. One downer person can affect the mood of a whole group and so can one upbeat person.

Ever wonder why that is so? It's because most of the systems in your body are closed loop, which means they are automated. They function without your conscious control. The limbic system is the emotional center, and it operates differently. The limbic system is an open loop system that depends primarily on external sources to manage itself. Your limbic system is impacted by the emotions of others. Indeed, both encouraging and demeaning emotions can spread like a cold between people and groups.

The process where a person can influence the emotions of others is called emotional contagion. We've all experienced this phenomena. This is when someone enters a room and everyone gets tense, or maybe the opposite occurs where one person's mood causes everyone to crack a smile. Professional speakers, lawyers, politicians, and actors are aware of emotional contagion. They choose certain words and use deliberate body language to keep people in their thinking brains, or not.

Refrain from engaging in conversations the trigger the survival brain: shaming, blaming, complaining, criticizing, comparing, repeating stories of woe, victim mentality, put downs, recycled disappointments, gossip, whining, angry outbursts, manufactured drama, and snide remarks.

I'm not suggesting your stifle yourself or anyone from speaking the truth. Gossip, whining, and complaining is natural to humans, but if it keeps us from accessing "thinking" brain, then it becomes a problem. When there's abuse or an injustice has occurred, it's essential not ask these people to "get over it" or stay optimistic in the heat of the moment. Feelings buried alive never die, so if you experience trauma, it is essential to find a safe place to be supported. Like I said earlier, this isn't about categorizing words, people, and events into positive and negative. It's about getting healthy and assisting others to do the same.

Try redirecting conversations toward topics that include learning, possibilities, empathy, solutions, preferred outcomes, best practices, success strategies, respectful humor, favorite stories, and inspiring ideas. This is key for political conversations, especially. Stay clear of labels that use "good" or "bad." Instead, discuss how you can become the change you want to see.

Can you hold your tongue if the conversation turns to gossip? Gossip is an unhealthy way that some rely on to form bonds. It has become our new small talk, and it is bad for us, our relationships, and our health. It often comes from a need for connection. When you want to break free from these interactions, you can change the subject, compliment the one who is being criticized, or you can simply leave. You can also just listen to this person with silent compassion for everyone involved. Remember, no one can "make" you feel a certain way. When you're aware of your thoughts and can choose them accordingly, little harm can touch you.

Start finding people who want to practice staying in high-quality, thinking brain conversations. Set a timer for 10-20 minutes and talk only about what you are looking forward to, what you'd like to see happen, favorite books and movies, people who inspire you, a dream vacation, what's going well in your life, or activities you enjoy.

Now that you have access to this rare scientific information, it's time to practice. Your progress won't be a sprint around the block; it's more of a marathon that requires your consistent awareness and endurance. The results, however, can be instantaneous. For many, it's the spark that launches them into a superior version of themselves. Their certainty and self-trust may be the biggest payoff of all.

If there's only one thing you take from this chapter, invite yourself to spend an extra minute or two in bed in the morning. In that time, create a picture of the day you would like to have. See your meetings and interactions play out with the best outcomes possible. Envision genuine smiles, clear boundaries, respectful behavior, and all the support you need for your destiny to unfold.

This is no different than what professional athletes do to prepare for competition. They see gratitude. You, too, can become a ruler of your response and a driver of your power. All you need to begin and maintain is already inside of you.

***

To contact Robin:

www.robinrose.com

503-873-3649

robin@robinrose.com

Molly McGee Hewitt

Molly McGee Hewitt, is a recognized speaker, author, consultant and trainer with over thirty years of experience. She currently serves as chief executive officer and executive director for the California Association of School Business Officials (CASBO).

Molly's career began as a public information officer and public relations professional. She has extensive experience dealing with the news media during turbulent times and has taught spokesperson/media training to professionals including school board members and administrators around the United States.

Molly's experience includes serving as a classroom teacher, administrator, and school board member. She was first elected to public office at the age of 19. She has worked with a variety of organizations in North, South and Central America. Molly is noted for her humor, her common sense approach to leadership and her ability to motivate and inspire her audiences and colleagues.

Molly has received over 200 awards and commendations for her public service and leadership She is the author of more than 14 books and publications. She also writes regular columns for CASBO's print and digital publications and is a frequent contributor of feature articles.

Molly's education includes a B.S. in Organizational Development M.S. in School Business Leadership. In 2017, she will receive her Ph.D.

"The E Factor:" The Power of Encouragement

By Molly McGee Hewitt

If you took a moment to ponder who or what has had the greatest impact on your life, would you identify it as a powerful encouragement or discouragement? Almost everyone I share this question with gives me the same answer – the people or events that have shaped their lives, their approach to leadership and their futures were powerful encouragers. These events and people pushed us forward. Some did so with positive encouragement and, on occasion, some with a lesson that enabled us to turn the corner and create a new destiny.

Reflecting on my life, the power of encouragement has played and continues to play a significant role. As a student, the teachers I remember the most were those who encouraged me, saw beyond who I was then and what I knew and helped propel me forward. As a teenager, I was drawn to positive role models and people who consistently and continually brought out the best in me and reminded me of what I could accomplish. As a young professional, those in leadership positions who encouraged me to try new things, to learn and grow, and to become more were powerful forces in my life. These forces were so significant that when I felt as if I had no personal power or was unsure of what I could accomplish or who I was, they propelled me forward.

The "E Factor," or encouragement plays a role in every life. In our families, we see it revealed in how we encourage and support each other and how we value and encourage our children. Strong families value, appreciate and respect each-others' talents. They want to see everyone reach their potential and live extraordinary lives. As a parent, each of my children are very different. They each have their own personalities, intellects, interests, and motivations. My job is to encourage them in whatever they choose and to help them to succeed. That may include seeing them for who they can become, and not who they are right now. The E Factor is about seeing beyond today and envisioning someone's tomorrow.

Not everyone is blessed with an encouraging family or situation. At times, someone's success or their attempts to try something new or different leads to discomfort and even sabotage. An old analogy of a crab pot comes to mind. When one crab tries to crawl out, other crabs reach out and bring them back down. For people in these situations, the power of encouragement can help free them of those barriers and help them move forward.

Teachers and those in authority positions with young people have a duty to practice the E Factor. Children and young adults are particularly and powerfully influenced by the words of those in authority or whose opinions they value. The classroom teacher who sees a student struggling and lends a hand, the scout leader who helps you to complete that event, the coach who pushes you to exceed your limits – each of them, through their words, behaviors and actions, influences those in their care.

Early in my career, I had the privilege of teaching elementary school for several years. Every year, I would eagerly await a new class of children. I would wonder who would appear in my classroom, what would I learn from them and what I would teach them. I knew deep in my soul that they would learn much more from me than the curriculum I would teach. They would watch me very carefully. They noticed what I wore, my shoes, my hair, my moods, my words and how I treated everyone in the class and at the school. They were watching me to determine several things. First, was I authentic? Did my words, actions, and behaviors match? Did I say one thing and do something different? Did I play favorites? Did I like the smartest kids most? Did I give more time and attention to some and not to others? Was I tired or energized? Was I happy, stressed, sad or in a bad mood? They were watching me to determine if my actions were authentic. If I was authentic, a bond formed almost instantly.

Those children taught me as well. I learned from them how powerful their encouragement was to me. A smile from a child, a hug when I needed it, a struggling student who become a scholar, a child acting up in the hope of garnering attention – I learned a great deal about human nature, motivation, love, and encouragement. They taught me that what I did was important, but that who I was, that was even more valuable.

Today, many of my former students are my friends. The power of social media allows me to reconnect with them and to continue to play a role in their lives. When they marry, graduate from college or graduate school, get a promotion or have a significant event, I get to share in their success and encourage them. When life is rough and they are struggling, I get another chance to offer my hand, my ear, or my resources to encourage them to continue. I am honored that they still value me as a friend and mentor.

Professionally, encouragement takes many forms in the workplace. Today more than ever, recruiting, hiring, training and retaining good employees is a priority for businesses. Turnover costs millions of dollars and can slow down an organization or company's progress and success. The cost impact extends from dollars to human capital. Recruiting the right employees today requires more than ads, it requires trying to make sure that the culture of your organization is a right fit for the prospective employee. Also, in today's market, employees often do their homework before applying or accepting a position. Most people are looking for fair compensation and benefits, but they also want to find a place where they and their skill sets will be welcome and valued.

The E Factor starts the moment a person applies for the job. How they are treated, how their application is acknowledged and how the recruitment process operates sends out a message of encouragement or discouragement. One applicant I interviewed told me that in one instance, the company he was applying for a position with was trying to find a reason not to hire him in the process. He felt they assumed he would not last or be the right candidate. When I questioned why he felt that way, he said, "I never thought they saw any value in me. I was so excited about the opportunity that I was willing to take a lesser job. After the interview, I would not have taken any job there." Upon more discussion, I found that the process was not user friendly and was based on identifying your weaknesses, not your strengths.

Onboarding is the term used today for the introduction and orientation of new employees and almost every article I have read about this practice validates the power of encouragement. When a new employee starts, welcome them to the team and ensure they have the tools they need to do their job well from the moment they arrive. Plan for their arrival and make sure they have an opportunity to meet their co-workers, celebrate their arrival and, from day one, make them feel they are a welcomed addition to the team.

Years ago, I went to work for a professional association in Los Angeles. On the first day of my job, I was greeted at the reception area by name, welcomed and escorted to my new office. At my desk, I was greeted with a floral arrangement, business cards, logo wear and a card from the executive director welcoming me to the association. I was given a moment to hang up my coat, and then I was given a tour of the office and introductions were made. Our final stop was the break room. The entire staff greeted me with coffee and donuts! I felt like a rock star. Later, my direct supervisor took me to lunch and shared with me significant policies and information I would need. At the end of my first day of employment, I knew I had made a great decision and was grateful to work for the group. The encouragement and welcome I felt that day have stayed with me for over 20 years!

Sadly, that was the only time in my career that I had this experience. Most times, when arriving at a new job, it seemed almost as if I was unexpected. I often had to hunt and scrounge for the office supplies I needed and to find out office protocols, I had to do research and put in a lot of effort. It often made me question the leadership of the organization and whether or not I was a good fit.

For the last 10 years, I've had the opportunity to put the E Factor to practice professionally. I remember that great experience early in my career and I work to duplicate it with new hires. I also strive to practice what I preach with my current staff. I recognize that being identified by name, being spoken to with respect, sharing success and disappointments, and compassion go a long way in establishing positive relationships and morale. My goal is to create a work place where every employee recognizes and practices the power of encouragement.

How can you put the E Factor into operation? Is it expensive, time consuming or difficult? The answer to all of this is NO. Not just no, but heck NO! The E Factor is not a product you buy or a program you sign up for. It's a philosophy and life practice. You start with mindfulness and a bit of forethought. You seize every normal event, activity or opportunity and bring encouragement to it. It's about changing your orientation to your world and deciding to make a difference.

Take email, for example. For some of us, it's a four-letter word. We get too much of it, people are too demanding with their requests and it seems to multiply by the minute. When we log in to our computers, instead of seeing encouragement, we see a challenge. One of my friends calls their email "evil mail." I see it differently. I receive a great number of emails each day, and they're not all thank you notes, invitations and congratulatory comments! I get requests, complaints, and a wide range of correspondence inquiries in my email. I look at my email as "E Tickets."

When I was a child, Disneyland had a ticket system for their rides in Anaheim. The tickets ranged from A to E. Upon entering the theme park, you were given a packet of tickets. The best tickets were the E tickets and they were for the most popular rides. There were also fewer E tickets than any other in the book. I can remember using our E tickets first and always coming home with an assortment of A, B, C and maybe even a D ticket or two! When I say E ticket, I remember the power of those early trips to Disneyland and the joy I got from those tickets. My E Tickets today are my email.

Your language and word choices are significant in your practice of encouragement. How we say what we want to say, the words we choose and the tone of our writing send messages. My goal is to create an E Ticket with every exchange of email or texts that I have. I try to communicate clearly, use positive and appropriate language and to meet the needs of the person sending the mail. I hope to leave them with a positive and encouraging email. I use words and phrases like please, thank you, I appreciate your time, your contribution is valuable, great hear from you, thank you for allowing me to comment and your help is valuable. I also choose to end my mails with phrases like with respect, you rock, thank you for your contribution, we can do this or warmly. Not only do I try to use this type of language – I mean it as I write it!

Every time the phone rings, it can be an interruption or an opportunity. I see it as an "E Moment." My voice, tone and demeanor will set the stage for our conversation. My goal is for you to hear me smile through the phone and to hear from my voice a positive and kindred spirit. When I greet folks in the morning, say good bye, or just stop to chat, I see these as "E Opportunities" to practice with I preach! Staff meetings, text messages, publications, speeches – each one is a chance to make a positive difference and a contribution to the organization. I also practice this with my family and friends.

The power of encouragement is a hallmark of great leaders. As a student and lover of history, I see examples of leadership in many forms. Not all of it is encouraging. Some leaders use fear as a motivator, others use bribes or negative consequences. The most powerful examples of great leadership are those who encourage others to achieve and succeed. When employees and colleagues of mine succeed, I am delighted and I feel much like I did in the classroom – I played a role in their success. Their success empowers and encourages me! Organizations and families are never built by one great leader, they are built by leaders who encourage and empower others to be leaders. For me, to succeed in leadership, I must help others to succeed as well.

Throughout my life, I have received encouragement in many forms and on numerous occasions. Some I have shared with you already from my classroom. When I have supervised and managed people or groups, I have felt their support and encouragement. When I ran for office at the age 18, and was elected at age 19, people I had never met applauded my efforts and encouraged me! Some showed that encouragement by action, some contributed money or time, they walked precincts for me, made phone call, held coffees and displayed yard signs. Some just shared their hopes and goals with me and encouraged me to make a difference.

Others have encouraged me by helping me to deal effectively with challenges or obstacles. When a project failed, when I was laid off, when my spouse or parent died, when I was ill or suffering from a loss of direction – they practiced the E Factor by being there for me. By listening, offering constructive and honest feedback, encouraging me to try again and reminding me of the possibilities that were ahead. They often gave me a perspective and an energy that I could not muster at the time. The E Factor in all of its forms! From written to verbal to a cooked dinner or a shared cup of coffee, the power of encouragement comes in many forms – all fit for the perfect occasions!

The E Factor is about using the power of your words, actions, and behaviors to encourage others. It can be as simple as an email or a phone call. It is not limited to our family, friends, or co-workers, but extends to everyone we with whom we interact, do business, or meet. From the barista at my local Starbucks, to the flight attendant on my trip, to the desk clerk, to the person introducing me before I speak, the E Factor is at work in my life. When I leave a tip for the maid in a hotel, I write a note of thanks and leave the money on top. An extra moment of effort to thank someone for what can be a thankless job! An extra tip or a note about great service is another example of an E Opportunity.

Like you, I live in the real world. Not everything is peaches and cream, and there are times when I must deal with poor service, underperforming employees, or the sticky wickets that life places before us. Practicing the E Factor and being a positive encouragement to others is possible even in trying times. In those moments, I am moved by compassion and my goal is to address the situation and to find a solution that benefits everyone. I have learned that truth and honesty are always a part of practicing the E Factor. When faced with these obstacles or challenges, I do not sugar coat them or act as if they are not there, I address them head-on and without rancor, personal attack, or anger. My words, actions and behaviors can and will empower me even in those situations.

Earlier, I mentioned that the E Factor starts with mindfulness. It does. It starts with an intention and a commitment to encouragement and to being an encouraging person to everyone and everything I encounter. It causes me to pause and reflect on myself first. I think about my words, my actions, my behaviors, my attitudes, my body language, my demeanor, and my intentions. I do not practice the power of encouragement for what I get from it, I practice it for who I become when I use it. I become a better person, mother, wife, colleague, and leader when I encourage others. I also become a person of personal integrity when my words, actions, philosophies, and behaviors are in alignment with this core value and belief.

Gratitude is a part of my life. I have been blessed with wonderful opportunities to speak, write, consult and to be a leader. I have traveled the world, studied under amazing leaders, and served wonderful organizations. The E Factor has been and will continue to be a guiding principle in my life, my faith, and my work. It can transform your life and enhance your leadership too! E, too?

***

To contact Molly:

MollyMcGeeHewitt@aol.com

916 955 5528

5 New Grafton Court, Suite 100

Sacramento, CA 95835

Sharissa Sebastian

Sharissa is a Career Success Coach for Ambitious Women, a speaker, author, contributor to Forbes and the Huffington Post, a member of Forbes' Coaches Council, a radio show host and co-owner of Stop. Smile. Breathe. Women's Retreats. Her passion is helping women get unstuck in their careers, have jobs they love and that compensates them well so they wake up excited and energized every day.

Mindset Makeover

By Sharissa Sebastian

Introduction

After all my ups and downs, here is what I know for sure…having a life you love comes down to three things—psychology, spirituality (not religion) and strategy. They are the connection between mind and behavior, your belief system, and the actions you take to get the results you want which creates a life to love. The intersection of these three areas determines how much joy and fulfillment life gives you.

You have a choice in every moment and the more you make those choices from a success mindset, the more likely you are to achieve what you want. Let's get started…

Overcoming Obstacles

The first thing we want to do is identify anything that may be standing in our way. An obstacle, in this context, is anything that could get in the way of you achieving what you'd like. It could be *internal* such as beliefs, thoughts, and assumptions; or *external* such as your environment, circumstances, or other people. The good news is that breaking through internal obstacles is powerful in helping you overcome any external limitations when you're committed to a goal that is important to you. For example, one of the biggest obstacles I had to overcome was to leave a stressful, unfulfilling, well-paying job to start my coaching business as a single mom. I felt fear – the fear of failure, of financial ruin, and of the unknown.

I took the leap despite these fears because the fear of staying the same became greater than the fear of change.

I had two BIG motivating factors. My motivation was my daughter and my desire to make a difference doing what I enjoyed. I also had faith and belief that God would lead me down the right path but I had to be intentional in seeking his guidance. I needed to look my challenges square in the face and be prepared with a game plan. I did that by asking myself empowering questions that focused on my motivating factors.

Here are three things to focus on to overcome anything that may hold you back:
1. *Have clarity on what you want.*
2. *Know exactly what your obstacles are.*
3. *Identify your motivational factors.*

The Power of Focus, Meaning and Action

Where focus goes energy flows. You tend to attract more of what you focus on. If you focus on lack and worry, you'll get more of that. If you focus on being excited about a great opportunity, you become more open and you will be inspired to take action towards it. You will feel better and more optimistic. The meaning you give every situation you are in or everything that happens to you is key. You will learn faster by having a positive outlook and you'll be better equipped for what you truly want.

Inspired action is critical.

Even if you're not sure, do something. Inaction and waiting for the right moment could keep you waiting forever! If it doesn't work out as planned, try something new, but never give up. Success favors the bold.

Affirmations

Affirmations are statements that you repeat to affirm a belief or a desired state. The key to effective affirmations is to include an emotional component. In other words, really feel what it would be like for the statement to be true. <u>Believe it and expect the outcome</u>.

Here are some affirmation statement examples…
- ✓ God's blessings flow to me in avalanches of abundance.

- ✓ I am confident and capable of handling anything that comes my way.
- ✓ I am a fantastic _____.
- ✓ I am extremely successful at my career.
- ✓ I value myself and spend time doing things I love.

Benefits to affirmation statements include protecting against the damaging effects of stress on your problem solving abilities; refocusing your mind to a more positive mindset when you find yourself slipping into negative self-talk and judgment; helping you feel better; having more confidence and performing more effectively.

Embracing Negativity

This simply means not fighting against unwelcomed emotions. You are going to experience this. The way to successfully navigate these emotions is to acknowledge them so you aren't consumed and kept from focusing on what's important. If you're angry, admit it without judgment. Ask yourself from a place of curiosity, not judgment, what could have triggered this emotion. Ask yourself what thoughts you were having that could have led to that feeling.

Your thoughts lead to your feelings which in turn affects your actions.

It's a challenge to refocus your mind but the more you replace negative thoughts with positive affirmations (with belief and the emotions associated with those statements) the faster you rewire your mind to the emotions you desire. The key is not simply to recite the words but to truly embody them and believe them to the point where it becomes second nature for your mind to go there and for you to feel better on a regular basis.

Language

Your internal dialogue plays a significant role in your emotions and your actions. Do you ask yourself questions like this when things don't seem to go your way? "Why does this always happen to me?" These are known as disempowering questions or thoughts. Here are some empowering questions to consider:

- ✓ What's great about this? (even though the situation may not be ideal)
- ✓ What can I learn from this?
- ✓ How can I use this experience to help others?
- ✓ What can I be grateful for in this moment?
- ✓ How can I use this to improve in some way?

I encourage you to come up with your own empowering questions to add to your tool belt. Practice awareness in those situations. If you notice your emotions starting to rise, take a moment to pause, be aware of what's going on internally and switch to asking yourself these questions. If you are committed to this, it will drastically reduce your stress levels. Promise!

What Are You Proud of Yourself for?

Reminding yourself of your accomplishments has several benefits. Not only does it help to boost your confidence and remind you what you're capable of, but it's also a great form of motivation. It can help you keep the momentum going to achieve what is important to you or it can help you overcome a challenge you may be facing. Keeping this list will also help you prepare for your performance reviews at work.

Just remember to do this with the intention of helping others vs being an ego boost which leans towards arrogance instead of confidence.

Belief

A belief is simply accepting something is true or that something exists. Your beliefs are what shape you and can often dictate the trajectory of your life from an early age. They influence your every decision so it's important to unpack this and discover just how they are helping or hurting you in achieving your goals. Your belief system and thoughts determine your emotions, which determine your actions, which ultimately determine your destiny. Here are some examples of empowering beliefs: 'Everything that happens to me also happens for me'. 'Every situation (good or bad) is an opportunity to learn, grow and get closer to my goal'. 'I believe that I always have the option of choosing gratitude in every situation'. What are some empowering beliefs you can choose to have to reduce your stress, help you focus and ultimate achieve the results you want?

Forgiveness

When you focus on regret, anger, frustration or any of those emotions tying you to your past, you waste energy that can be better used to help you be more present and move towards the future you really want. If you have a difficult time forgiving someone (possibly yourself), these are six important things to remember to forgive someone (including yourself).

Six Important Points of Forgiving People

1. Remember everyone does the best they can in a given moment. If you find yourself judging others, don't judge yourself! Notice the thought and let it go and choose to focus on something positive.

2. Every person and encounter happens for a reason. Ask yourself what you can learn from this, even though it hurts.

3. How important is this in the grand scheme of things? You can choose to reframe it and learn from it so you can let go of the hurt and pain.

4. Forgiveness is challenging. Try to have compassion for others. It's also important to recognize when a relationship is toxic and it's best to set boundaries rather than constantly ending up in the same cycle.

5. When asking for forgiveness from someone, being vulnerable is valuable. A great deal of healing takes place when you allow

yourself to be vulnerable and share how you feel vs blaming the other person.

6. Don't take it personally. Easier said than done, I know! Remember, holding onto anger is like drinking poison and expecting the other person to die. You can choose to let these moments shape you or break you.

Here's a good way to start to release what may be holding you back. Write down everything you need to forgive others and yourself for (without judgment). Then recite the following:

> *"I realize that harboring anger, regret, frustration, and any negativity from the past is not serving me. I am ready to release this, forgive myself and others for everything on this list, and finally break free from_____ so I can focus on what is really important. As I do this, I feel completely relieved of this burden and ready to move forward and focus on what's really important to me."*

Every time you feel those emotions or memories resurfacing, remember that exercise and simply say, "I release this" and shift your focus to something positive.

Faith, Trust and Letting Go

When you take inspired action, you need to trust that things are going to work out for you. It may not always be easy or perfect but all things work in your favor even if everything doesn't happen exactly according to your plan. The second part of this is surrender. When you've done what you can, surrender your desire and know that what's meant to happen will happen for you.

Surrender is not easy but the more you trust and focus on letting go of what you can't control the less stressed you are and the more easily those opportunities seem to be attracted to you. God is good, God is love (He adores you) and God is in control. You may call the power greater than yourself by another name like the universe, source, or something else. The concept of having faith that everything happens for a reason and you are supported is the same.

Visualization, Stillness and Meditation

When you think of a big goal or dream that you want to achieve it's natural to think of all of the obstacles that will come your way. The problem is far too often we allow these obstacles to become so big in our minds that it stops us from moving forward and we settle for mediocrity.

The truth is if you can't picture yourself achieving a goal chances are you won't. The more vivid you can get, the better it will work for you. Spend about 5 to 10 minutes picturing yourself achieving each one. Picture what you will do once your goal is reached using your five senses.

Meditation is another great practice to help you clear your mind, focus, and get inspired into action towards what you really want and what's best for you. If you've been hesitant to meditate and you think it's difficult or may not work for you, remember this…if you can worry, you can meditate! Meditation is simply focusing on something.

Gratitude

Studies show that people who regularly practice gratitude by taking time to notice and reflect upon the things they're thankful for, experience more positive emotions, feel more alive, sleep better, express more compassion and kindness and even have stronger immune systems. The more you're genuinely grateful, the more you'll have to be grateful for. You can't be truly grateful and angry or stressed at the same time so this is a great way to get in a positive frame of mind to eliminate those energy-sapping negative vibes!

Giving Back

Everyone knows the importance of giving back and making a difference in this world. You may have heard the secret to living is giving.

Here are some benefits of helping others...
1. It connects you with like-minded people.
2. It gives you a chance to select an area where you can get more experience.
3. It can be the inspiration you're seeking for your next career opportunity.
4. It's a great way to get experience in an area you already have interest in.

There are many ways to do give back, such as volunteering for projects at work, community service projects, joining organizations, or even volunteering with a group of friends. As long as your intentions are sincere and you're looking to be of service more than to be rewarded, you will get great benefit from this!

The Power of Presence

The way you present yourself is closely related to the way you feel, your confidence and the way you are perceived. If you want to feel empowered try some power poses focus on improving your posture; shoulders back, head up, smile more and make eye contact with others. I encourage you to listen to this Ted Talk by Harvard scientist, Amy Cuddy, on the importance of body language. I also recommend her New York Times bestselling book "Presence."

Intention and Inspired Action

The basis of an intention is to have a purposeful goal or objective. The clearer you are on what you would like to achieve and why it is so important to you, the higher the likelihood of you achieving it.

In order to have a strong intention it's important to realize the significant role belief plays in it. The more you believe that you will achieve what you will set out to, the stronger the intention. You will move towards what you focus on so it's important to be intentional with your goals and have a strong, compelling reason why achieving it is a must.

Vision Boards

In addition to visualization, creating a vision board is a great, fun way to get clarity on what you want and imprint those pictures in your mind daily to get you motivated and moving in that direction quickly. Here are some easy steps to do this:

1. Purchase a board (I used a cork board)
2. Some material to secure your pictures to the board, like pushpins or glue dots
3. Magazines or printed images
4. Post It notes
5. Get Creative!
6. I like to cut out the pictures and categorize them (for example, giving, family, travel, business, etc.).
7. I also use the Post It notes to add affirmations or to note anything else I'd like to experience during the year (joy, peace, love, abundance, etc.).
8. Have fun putting everything together on your board!

I like to do this exercise with my daughter once a year. We usually have a vision board party on New Year's Eve. We put music on, grab some snacks and have fun! You want to place the board in a place where you know you will look at it often. You may even want to add this to your morning or evening routing.

Here is a personal story (one of many) of the power of visualization and intent...

One of the photos on my vision board is of Arianna Huffington and her 12 secrets to Thrive. I looked at it every night and thought that I would love to share information that would have that level of impact. I took inspired action and within a few months I received an email from Arianna saying that she would love for me to be a contributor for the Huffington Post. You can read my articles for the Huffington Post on my blog page here:

http://sharissasebastian.com/blogpage/

Support Team

Jim Rohn has a great quote that goes like this:

"You are the average of the 5 people you spend the most amount of time with."

It's incredibly important to surround yourself with people who lift you up, support you without judgment and have your best interest at heart. Take a quick evaluation of who your tribe is and ask if they're helping you to be the best you can be, or not. It's important to not only find people who will support you but also those who you can contribute to.

In addition to close family and friends, you may want to add a mentor, colleague, or coach to your support team. You can find like-minded people at Meetup groups, places of worship, volunteer opportunities, at work, or through LinkedIn to name a few places. It's critical to have these people in your tribe. None of us can achieve what we truly desire alone.

Conclusion

Mindset mastery is a journey and not a destination. When you are committed to making these small shifts daily, you begin to experience stronger relationships and more peace, joy, clarity, compassion, confidence and courage. My hope for you is that you find what truly sets your soul on fire and commit to pursuing that with everything you've got so you can be of the most service to others in a way that brings you immense joy.

To your happiness and success!

***

To contact Sharissa

www.sharissasebastian.com

Susan Sharp

Susan Sharp speaks and writes about creativity and living a creative life. An Assistant Professor of Theatre at Carl Sandburg College in Galesburg, Illinois, Susan is also a keynote speaker, playwright, singer/songwriter, abstract artist and Color Code Certified Independent Trainer. Susan's research on creativity and personal giftedness has made her a sought-after speaker and workshop leader. From keynote addresses on finding your creative drive, to workshops on interpersonal communication or utilizing the gifts of your staff, Susan thrives on helping organizations to discover their strengths and gifts. Creative problem-solving and innovation are key areas of interest for Susan and she was recently a part of a European study on creative thinking. Her podcast and newsletter, *Create Yourself*, have a loyal audience.

Susan is a member of numerous speaking and art organizations including The National Speaker's Association, The Illinois Theatre Association and The Surface Design Association. She holds a Master's degree from The University of Northern Iowa, a Bachelor's degree from St. Ambrose University and an executive certificate from Notre Dame.

You're Already a Masterpiece
By Susan Sharp

I. Artists see possibilities

There is a fascinating video online that shows how a nail is suspended in the middle arm of an E-shaped cut of wood with the nail touching neither the top or bottom arm. At first glance it appears that natural laws have been suspended or some sort of magic is at play. Logic would have it that one of the ends must have been glued on after the nail was driven in or that the nail was actually in two pieces glued on either side of that middle arm. But the wood smith assures us it is made from one solid piece of wood and that the nail is driven through it. How was it done? Another example shows a golf ball rolling around in the middle of a wood cube. How could this be possible? And of course there is the age-old mystery of a ship in a bottle. Is it creative engineering, deceitful manipulation or an optical illusion? When you learn how the nail is driven in that piece of wood, you look at things differently. You begin to wonder what else is possible. You start thinking like an artist.

Artists ponder possibilities all the time as they manipulate materials to achieve a desired effect. Artists push the boundaries of their materials and imaginations as they experiment, fail, try again and so forth until they achieve. And for an artist, the pursuit of creating a great piece is just as fun as achieving it. I think of American glass sculptor Dale Chihuly whose work is all about manipulating molten glass with movement, tools and air in a very short window of time before it must be thrust back into the fire or surrendered to a permanent state. We don't call him deceitful or an illusionist, we call him an artist; he manipulates materials. He can predict with a high certainty how each movement will affect the glass. Even with all that skill and expertise, there is still shattered glass on the floor at the end of the day. Is he a failure? No, we call that practice. And tomorrow the pursuit continues. When Dale lost his left eye in a car accident, he enlisted the help of others to do the glass blowing. And when a shoulder injury made him unable to hold the pipe, he continued to create while he encouraged and advised. He liked the new perspective and found another chapter in his artistry, and a myriad of faithful, happy students wanting to study with the master. Is he less of an artist because his hand isn't on the glass blowing pipe? Who directs it however? Completely hands off, through his coaching and encouragement, he is still making art; still breathing air into the creative process.

I am an artist and work in many areas. I am a playwright, theatre director, keynote speaker, a singer/songwriter, and voice-over artist among other things. I enjoy home improvement, interior decorating and I am an abstract artist. Each of these endeavors requires the manipulation of materials. In plays I manipulate words to achieve a desired effect. As a director, I help actors with inflection, dialects, body positioning and timing to achieve a particular tone or feel to their characters. As a singer I use vibrato, or swing the melody or emphasize certain beats or words in my interpretation of a song, and as an abstract artist, I enjoy color and texture and finding sources for those in unusual materials like natural dyes or old billboard vinyl.

When I go to art shows I walk around and take in the beauty and mystery of each piece. With wide-eyes and curiosity, I ponder how the unique look was achieved and I have a conversation with it trying to understand its process. And because I do a myriad of artistic things, I find the art within a play and the theatre within art and the rhythm in the fabric I'm sewing. When you live an artistic life there are many synapses in the brain firing at once. And materials speak to me. I have entire conversations in my head as I ponder what's possible. The madness of artists is really a hyper-aware, turbo-charged emotional mind negotiating a thousand ideas at once.

Whether it's through the countless hours of practice in manipulating one material like Chihuly or in constant experimentation with multiple materials, an artist comes becomes one with them. If you watch skilled painters they often hold their pencils and pens in a unique way. After thousands of hours of learning and using various techniques the rest of their hand-tasks are affected. The brush is an extension of the hand and more importantly the eyes and the mind. The materials in which artists work become extensions of self.

II. See yourself as a work of art

When I was young, I wanted to be the next Nadia Comaneci. My dad, a professional floor installer, covered a 2 x 4 in carpet pad and it became my balance beam in the backyard. It didn't matter that it was on the ground and not in the air, that it was not regulation length or width--it was a symbol of my dream. I watched gymnastics on television and I loved the leotards, the camaraderie, and the determination of those tiny spitfire girls. I wanted to be a part of that scene!

The difficulty with that dream, apart from being totally uncoordinated, was that it came with a 7-year olds perspective. At 7, anything was possible. If I could have been objective and had the ability to take stock of my gifts, I would have seen that I only loved the spotlight, I didn't love the sweat and effort to get *in* the spotlight. I would have also seen that I was not very athletic and I was not gutsy. But I could write the dream, play act the dream, dress up the dream, stage the dream—in these I was fearless. That was more appealing than the dream itself. Even in my short-lived pursuit of gymnastics gold, I was given great insight into myself. But it was not until years later that I would find value in having day-dreamed about gymnastic stardom as a stepping stone to my career in the theatre.

The first verb in the Bible is the word *created*. Genesis 1:1 says, "In the beginning God created the Heavens and he Earth." God is a creative God and his first recorded action was to create. Genesis 1:27 goes on to say, "So God created man in his own image." If this is true and we believe that God is complete and lacking nothing, then we have to conversely believe *we* are complete. We are not broken, incomplete or lacking. If you then pursue an education and learn new skills and grow your outlook you are doing so from a position of power, not weakness. You are pursuing a further understanding of the gifts that you were given and how they might serve the world. But like my 7-year old self, we are distracted by the numerous focus-stealing parts of life. We stray from understanding ourselves to *fulfilling* ourselves—it becomes about what we *want* rather than who we *are*. I wanted to be a gymnast, but that is not what I was born for, that is not what I was equipped for. Could I still have been a gymnast? Yes. If I had been willing to sacrifice a lot, I believe I could have done it. But other factors like money, time, my attention span and my resilience level simply confirmed what was true—that was not my path.

We must make a shift in our thinking about our mission in life. We tell people they can be anything they want. Is that really true? Shouldn't we consider more than our desires? Shouldn't we also consider that for which we are uniquely equipped? A better message might be to find the answers to three questions:

1. What do you excel at/ what are your gifts?
2. What brings you joy?
3. How can it serve others?

> "At the intersection where your gifts, talents & abilities meet a human need, therein you will discover your purpose."
> Frederick Buchner.

One of the great joys of teaching is to confirm for students their gifts or to show them they have gifts where they thought they had none. I've received letters, emails and messages from students years later to say thanks for coaxing out my talents or for turning me onto a part of myself I didn't even know was there. Those letters never get commonplace for me—I have each one in a folder and I pull them out when I feel like I've failed and remind myself that I am still a work in progress. I have stumbled, not always served students the best I could, but learned from it, regrouped and vowed to do better for future students.

A few years ago I had an Army Veteran in my public speaking class who was gregarious, quick to laugh and to give people a good-natured ribbing. He said I used big words he'd never heard before and he loved my quirky sense of humor. He was in my office frequently and we would talk politics and life. A non-traditional student, he had seen the world, combat, and understood what it was like to lose buddies to war. He kept me on my toes that semester and I had come to really value his outlook on life and his easy-going nature. The last day of finals I didn't have any exams so I stayed home to grade papers, undistracted. He was moving after graduation the next day and had stopped in to say goodbye. I wasn't there. My officemate was and told me he wanted me to know he stopped. Within that same hour he died in an accident. You can imagine how I felt when I learned that he was gone. If I had been there would he have lingered in my office and avoided the accident? Would I have finally gone to have a beer with him like he had asked me more than once? That what-if game is a hard one; no one wins. One day each year I celebrate his life with my officemate, having a beer in his honor. And there's not a week that goes by that I don't think of him—a small token he gave me is still on my desk. I am better for having known him. For all his questions, I am a better professor. I grew because of him—professor taught by student. It's harder to get through that story when I give keynote addresses because we all know the sting of regret and sorrow and I feel it well up when I speak of him. We can all relate to missing our mark, our calling or our purpose. We can all relate to losing our tempers, our focus, or important people. We can relate to being dragged astray by the distractions of the world. And then we have to go back to the three questions above and remind ourselves what we're doing. If he were alive I believe my student would tell me to keep fighting the good fight. And I think he'd chuckle knowing he got in my head and has stayed.

III. You're already a masterpiece

Failure is a time to re-examine what led us to a particular point. Unfortunately, I see a lot of people who use failure as an indication that they lack something. We conclude failure is a character flaw or a lack of education or gifts. We convince ourselves we need something that we don't already have before we can move forward. Let me reassure you, you are complete as you are. You come into the world already a masterpiece. Your life's purpose is not to complete yourself—you are already complete. Your life's work is not to fix others—they are already whole. Your life's work is not to improve upon God's creation—He doesn't need your help.

There is a type of Japanese pottery called Kintsukoroi. Translated it means "to repair with gold." Broken pottery is mended with veins of gold lacquer making the broken piece more beautiful than the original. Even though we are whole, we sometimes feel broken. Just like the pottery, out of those feelings of brokenness can come something beautiful. Take time to ask yourself the three questions again. I find what's often lacking is that I'm neglecting #3, serving others. Ouch. That's hard to admit. How easy is it to become self-absorbed? Don't turn inward, reach out to others. When you give you get more in return. You can get an education or learn a skill or enlarge your thinking, but don't do so out of the need to complete yourself; do it out of the desire to *grow* yourself. Maybe you conclude that's just semantics, but if you believe you're complete, you act like it. And there is power in that view of self.

What do you sacrifice for? I know some book-lovers who would rather buy books than eat. I know some artists who say, "Give me canvas or give me death!" What can't you avoid doing? I cannot avoid creating—whether it's writing plays or songs, or art, sewing or singing or crafting a speech—I wander into creating something every day because that is where my natural instincts and intuition take me. The artistic process and mindset is at my core; it's what I do. I sleep sometimes only three hours a night because I'm in a creative zone. As Cecile B. DeMille said, "Creativity is a drug I cannot live without!"

When people learn the myriad of my creative pursuits they often confide that they aren't very creative or they wish they could be more creative. I try to give a little pep talk about believing in self and experimenting to get better, but most people have resigned themselves to thinking they're either born with a creative gene or they're not. Toward what do you naturally gravitate? Therein might reside your purpose. Creativity is a practiced, self-discipline; it is not only an innate gift. We are born with various levels of innate giftedness but how we nurture or neglect it determines if it grows. Relationships are the same way—there might be a natural connectedness but you can nurture or neglect it by how little time or respect you give others. We have all killed or seriously injured relationships for one reason or another. Creativity, like relating, is practiced. Creativity can be nurtured or neglected.

The intersection of the three questions is our purpose. Many people might have the same purpose in life, but you still have a unique calling. We get adversely hung up on the idea of being original or unique and conclude that we don't have anything unique to offer the world because we do something very similar to many others. Even if you repeat jobs or ideas uttered by others, how many people heard the original idea? For some percentage of your audience, *you* are the original source! Pablo Picasso said, "Art is theft." William Ralph Inge said, "What is originality? Undetected Plagiarism." And I stole both those quotes from Austin Kleon's 2012 book, *Steal Like an Artist*. As Ecclesiastes 1:9 says, "...there is no new thing under the sun." But there are new arrangements, combinations and patterns of ideas. I have coined this The Amalgamation Effect and I'm currently working on a book detailing this concept. And someone else may have already written one. So goes life. But I'll write the book anyway. And it will be unique in how it combines ideas.

Sometimes our thoughts must be redirected to see the truth of our giftedness and our purpose. We can never be objective about self and we are often our own worst enemy. But will you dare to view yourself as a masterpiece that is whole and complete with a unique voice for the world? Will you allow your viewpoint of self to be like that of an artist who sees a stack of raw materials and equates it to a great big pile of possibility?

The secret to the nail in the E-shaped piece of wood is really about seeing what's possible in the impossible. By soaking one end of the wood in boiling water and using a vice grip to compress it, a nail can be driven in the middle arm. Replace the wood into the boiling water and you can bend it back to its original shape, creating the illusion.

We too can be molded by hot water, failures, or the giftedness we have within us. We can feel broken and be mended even more beautifully. We can see unique arrangements of ideas as our originality and we can admit faults and see truths that confirm the masterpiece that lies within each of us.

***

To contact Susan:

You can learn more about Susan's work and speaking availability by visiting

www.ASharpDifference.com.

Susan's art and handmade items can be seen at www.pinoodles.etsy.com or www.asharpcontrast.etsy.com.

Harry Nichols

Harry Nichols is a Master Trainer of Neuro-Linguistic Programming, (co-founder Mastery of Deep Trance States®), Hypnotherapist, Master Hypnotist, and High Performance Coach. He has studied and delivered the cutting edge communication skills in the business and personal development field, for over 20 years. He has worked in the UK, Europe, United States, Canada and Central America.

He is known as a Master Change Facilitator helping individuals, groups and teams achieve the changes and results they over all improving productivity and achieving the highest standards of success.

Harry continues to upgrade his expertise in the areas of business, personal development and growth. Facilitating solution based strategies for individuals and organizations success is one of the premier goals of Thought Models Training.

Thought Modeling - The Heart Gateway Approach
By Harry Nichols

The whole idea of personal development and personal empowerment is one of today's most compelling subjects that propels our lives here in the 21st century. The relentless pursuit of achieving our personal goals can sometimes create it own challenges. Deciding on which area or areas to focus on can lead you to disappear down the personal rabbit hole of inertia.

Of course personal development is a life-long pursuit (even if in some cases it only lasts for the first few weeks or months after January 1 of any given year now, or in the future). And once you commit and take action in that direction then numerous choices become available to you. You can choose then to harness your personal empowerment and bridge the gap in between the life your living and the life you want to create.

The trend over the past few years has been interesting to observe and being in the business of personal and professional development for over 20 years, quite revealing. In this age of information overwhelm the idea of 'Hacking' makes for another variation of a recurring theme. There are a plethora of tools available the sheer volume of techniques are more than any one person could study in a lifetime.

Essentially I think it's all about goal setting, and how you define and approach what you want to achieve. It's all about growth, personal growth and defining, what that is and how you can get it. Your definition is the key to achieving your results!

There has been a detectable general shift from Brain/Mind focused communication to a more Heart focused communication style, which is very pleasing. The term 'Heart Centered' is appearing more and more in our everyday language. Granted whenever the word Heart is verbalized in general conversation, it does evoke some stereotypical responses. When the word heart is used in personal and business type, learning communication environments it takes a little framing and context to appreciate the full ramifications of how powerful 'Heart Centered' can change the very nature of the communication in a rather profound way.

The Journey

After many years on our continued journey of personal development and empowering we (my wife and business partner, Katherine and I) began to really embrace the idea of really working on how our thoughts create our reality. This became a commitment to deciding to learn more about exploring and experiencing our own inner deep states. It all began in earnest 9 years ago. The voyage of learning how to navigate the deeper regions of our minds and body as well as the world around us has been fun. The other side of this is that it has been quite a challenge.

However, our experiences have gathered a rich tapestry of processes that we think are very useful the in realm of personal development.

The consumption of human potential and personal development material has been ever growing throughout the past decades. As travelers along this path, we too have consumed voracious amounts from the vast libraries of knowledge available today.

In those years, we tried this, tried a little of that, we sought out the teachers, fallen deep inside the techniques, played with the mindsets, and sometimes not willingly, surrendered our bodies to the methods. We encountered many shifts and changes along the way. Studying the past, learning the new, seeking the ancient, embracing the modern, contemplating the contemporary and thoroughly trusting the future.

Whether it be knowledge from the East or the West, mind, body or spirit, one thing has become very clear; the answers lay in deep inside (and always have). The movement from the external to the internal has been our greatest joy. The hidden places and spaces, inside; and today's world, outside; has made our "education" in these matters literally one of a joyous reunion with myth, metaphor, science, the heart, the mind, the body and spirit (whatever that means to you). We listen not to the news of the day, but to the NEWS of each day as it shares its adventure with us.

We have embraced the passion and the joy, and as it has become our way of living, we began to notice the differences in our lives. We appear to be traveling "against the traffic" now. We seem to be able to traverse the bottleneck, things open, we go to places and sometimes we discover what people haven't noticed yet. We aim to manifest effortlessly, simply and without fear.

And it's not by design, but rather by *a design* we seem to be following without conscious awareness. It has a lovely feeling of "rightness". When we are not experiencing the feeling we know its time to STOP and wait and find the way to access that feeling again.

Learning how to listen to the deep resonance of the heart and the unconscious self, no matter where we are or who we are with is the key. Learning to 'Know Thyself' remains something of a cliché, yet dare I say personal development and personal empowerment is that very process in action.

No longer is the new frontier, "Somewhere out there" but in fact, it is and always has been "inside here. As one of my wise teachers once shared with me "the most successful people in this game of life, are those who learn to navigate their inner territory and bring back with them the wisdom and the tools to manifest a meaningful experience".

These ideas can sometimes meet with a bit of resistance in a boardroom setting or a high performance coaching scenario or even when you think about how you want to develop yourself and meet your personal goals. Start with your beliefs, values and definitions, this is where the work begins, starting with a solid foundation.

For the most part, in my experience we as humans tend to complicate the obvious, just because we can. When an individual (or group) has the opportunity to learn the obvious about what is simple, they become almost child-like again as they allow their own unique creative response to reach into the moment and create. With whatever approach you choose to navigate with, we all strive to make our experiences, measurable, accountable, successful and repeatable.

Thought Modeling

Even though we inhabit in our bodies physically, more often than not I've found a lot of people I meet are perpetually inside their head, or are held captive within the movies of the mind.

None of us make decisions based on reality itself. We make decisions based on our beliefs about reality. The entire world in its current configuration has a structural belief, you will need to change your beliefs in some way to realize success in the way you want as part of the process. Whether its personal development or development in any area of your life, your beliefs and values are vital in your continued growth.

The clear definitions of your belief structure at the root of your internal map of the world will prove to be the beginning of way to navigate your successful journey of experience.

This structure, which we create in the moment, very much embraces the models of thought. If it can be thought then it can be created, the thought itself is like a mini universe, so each thought has the creative power in universal design and if you consider this in everything you do you will have an idea of how this process works.

First it must come to thought, and then it must run through the whole of our system to support of the thought and then of course it must run through the physical being and if it does not reach too much opposition in any one of these filtering systems the thought has an opportunity to actually become or evolve.

Thought is a choice, for we must choose a thought and stay with it. Hence determination, hence much of language comes through thoughts and the desire to share thoughts whether internally or externally requires language.

So language patterns are part of Thought Modeling and will continue to be so, language existed in a variety of different ways. Language was often a part of the structure that evolved through no actual vocal expression. Eventually that too was a thought, to use the voice, to use the voice for more than a grunt, to give meaning to each grunt and eventually the grunt tonality and eventually of course verbal expression.

So in each evolution or stage of mankind's evolution a thought and thought models have been an essential part of where we as race are headed.

Therefore, in the creation of your development plan, you can bring in this aspect, you can look for the simplest way, the clearest way, the neatest way, the least challenging way and even if something is becoming a challenge in the moment. Stop yourself step back from it and say is there an easier way to do this.

How you think about something is how you will create it. You have to continue to keep thinking the same thoughts in order to create the same experience. In each and every endeavor the continual creation of the thought or the continual revisiting of the material that created the thought has to be re-anchored over and over again, in order to hold the model in place. When that thought model is in alignment with your positive beliefs you will begin to literally live your creation.

There are of course some aspects of current thinking that will need re-structuring, some of it is to simply bring it to awareness, and some of it is to actually re-write internal programs. There are internal programs running that do not support positive outcomes and need to be re-written because they continue to play and create a chaotic experience rather than a smooth and effortless one.

Simply bringing them to consciousness can assist in moving to disarm, some of the patterns that have been holding you back and will assist you in greater evolution with quicker results.

You see what you think is what you create, so if you believe something is unfair and you continue to move to support that belief, then of course everything around it, is going to move in that direction.

Energy Systems

Now as we worked with the principles of Thought Modeling, we began to incorporate many different and diverse modalities. The flow of information was sometimes overwhelming however the movement from this is just work to this is the way we live was exciting if challenging. We threw ourselves into our quest for personal growth utilizing our physical bodies as a perfect way to discipline our minds.

The modality that worked beautifully for us is Chi Gung, the ancient Chinese practice that met all our criteria and organically began to quiet our minds in support of our Thought Models.

I cannot speak highly enough for the incorporation of Meditation as part of your daily ritual, the practice of Meditation has significantly improved my ability to have a clear mind in everything I do.

Every morning doing chi gung and meditation is a wonderful way to start the day. The more we focused on our mind and body, the more we wanted to learn and the more we were led into the idea of energy systems and how they affect our well-being.

Let's face everything is energy and our studies led us into realm of Bioenergetics. Bioenergetics is a form of body-work, based upon the work of Wilhelm Reich. It can also be termed as a very specific kind of body psychotherapy, which is based upon the continuity between body and mind. Well the continuity between body and mind is right down our street. Learning is so much fun, when your open to possibilities of holistically developing yourself. The world is full of wonderful teachers of so called energy work and you can get lost in the shear volume of wisdom available.

The idea of energy systems these days brings up a lot of debate especially in and around the personal training and fitness arena. In the same way Energy Systems and the eastern systems of energy medicine brings up much debate in the medical community. Our way of navigating through these areas of contention goes back to our original premise on our journey. "What's important about developing myself personally? ".

What are our beliefs and values and how do we define them, in order to achieve our goals?

History, written or spoken, is indeed a construct of the writer or the orator. Just take a moment and marvel at how the beliefs of individuals, groups of individuals have shaped the now moment of this planet's perceived history. Even now the beliefs individually and collectively of the human race, shape the reality we live in. Beliefs so powerful that can propel man into the stars; yet put into jeopardy the longevity of our species. That can strive to prolong life and yet end it in the same breath without a second thought.

Beliefs dictate what responses we make to the world; the ways in which beliefs are validated act as a self-fulfilling prophecy. Even prior to the selection of response, the choice is often removed because the belief itself is synonymous with a perceptual filter that allows you to only notice parts of the world that are consistent with the belief you already have. As the man said, "If I hadn't believed it, I wouldn't have seen it." How you define a problem is going to determine how you deal with it. People make reality out of definition.

The Heart Gateway

As I continued along this personal development pathway, I began notice as one does, especially when you work in the facilitation field, therapy, coaching, communication skills, etc. That your clients often mirror where you are in your evolution, or point you in the direction you need to pay attention to.

Have you ever noticed when you ask people to point to self, they point to their heart space? When you talk about yourself you unconsciously identify with that space in between your breastbone. I also began to notice, when in it came from de-motivated clients, a key phrase, linguistically would consistently be verbalized would be "My heart's really isn't in it"

Then there was the occasion when Katherine and I attended 2 workshops and one talk, over a 3-week period, here in Vancouver, British Columbia, Canada. One was about exploring Brain/Mind States, one was about Body Work, and the third was about Spirituality. They cumulatively had a catalyzing effect on us. The profound common denominator in all three sessions, was role our heart plays in the mechanics of our consciousness. In fact, at the end of the 3rd workshop the spiritual one, I got to have a moment with the Tibetan Ripoche who facilitated our experience. He looked up me and down and said "Love More, Teach More, not from Here, but from Here" as he pointed first at my head, then my heart with a big smile on his face.

Suffice to say I got the message and really began to explore the heart and it's function in our body and our life. (Now let's not go into how he knew I was a teacher of sorts… that's another thing.) These nuggets led us even more deeply us into a powerful realm of study and practice through ancient wisdom, modern medicine, scientific research and personal experience. The Heart's Code, by Dr. Paul Pearsall is one of many great resources out there for understanding more about the heart.

The Ancient Egyptians, when they mummified their bodies after death, kept the physical heart and discarded the brain. It seems that the heart is the first organ to form during development of the baby, then the eyes, later on the brain. Our heart collects 100% of the energy accrued by our system, then distributes it through our nervous system. 40% of that energy goes to the brain. The miracle of nature that we are as human beings, just begged the question there's more going on here than we 'think'.

As humans we are a 'state of the art' system, which is constantly evolving and the more you look, the more you'll find our heart is much more than a pump, it is at the center of the system. Not only that when you truly delve into the science and all areas of study of us as human beings. You will find that we are 'State of the Art Complementary'. And our 'State of the Art Complementary' is communicating all the time. Our heart and our brain are not in conflict or opposition, in fact they are always seeking collaboration and harmony.

The heart is more than just a pump; it conducts the cellular symphony that is the very essence of our being – Dr. Paul Pearsall.

So with the understanding of the importance of our heart and its ability to communicate on many levels, our journey into the inner realms continues. Armed with this information our Thought Modeling has taken on more powerful significance, fueling our personal development growth. We've also noticed over the past few years there's been a slight shift to more and more heart centered approaches in all areas of business and business development strategies.

In our work, we are getting positive results, through this approach across the board with personal and client based solutions. If you choose to commit to life-long personal development, then find out what you really want. Define your positive beliefs and values, set realistic goals and commit to seeking an organized, easy to follow, educational system that creates a map to follow. It always helps to contemplate on what your heart thinks, because when you do, it's almost… Spiritual.

***

To contact Harry:

Harry Nichols

Master Change Facilitator

Master Trainer, Neuro Linguistic Programming

High Performance Coach

Master Hypnotist

Hypnotherapist

Telephone: 1 604 421 1722

www.thoughtmodels.com

https://www.facebook.com/deeptrancestates.mastery

https://www.facebook.com/thoughtmodels/?fref=ts

https://www.linkedin.com/in/harry-nichols-733476/

Skype: thoughtmodels

Afterword

Life is always a series of transitions… people, places, and things that shape who we are as individuals. Often, you never know that the next catalyst for change is around the corner.

Jim Britt and Jim Lutes have spent decades influencing individuals to blossom into the best version of themselves.

Allow all you have read in this book to create introspection and redirection if required. It's your journey to craft.

The Change is a series. A global movement. Watch for future releases and add them to your collection. If you know of anyone who would like to be considered as a co-author for a future book, have them email our offices at support@jimbritt.com.

The individual and combined works of Jim Britt and Jim Lutes have filled seminar rooms to maximum capacity and created a worldwide demand.

The blessings go both ways, as Jim and Jim are always willing students of life. Out of demand for life-changing programs and events, Jim and Jim conduct seminars and keynote presentations worldwide.

To Schedule Jim Britt or Jim Lutes as your featured speaker at your next convention or special event, or to organize and host a seminar in your area, email: support@jimbritt.com

Master your moment as they become hours that become days.

Your legacy awaits.

All the best,

Jim Britt and Jim Lutes

www.JimBritt.com

www.LutesInternational.com